Lost Sheep Publishing

The one always matters

Table of contents

Fear no more

Fear is an emotion, victory is your inheritance.

Fear no more

INTRODUCTION

Fear. Something that I know all too well. I know it in all shapes and in all sizes. Fear of stepping outside of my door, agoraphobia, check. Fear that cripples you so much that you're unable to move, check. The list is long. Panic attacks, agoraphobia, anxiety, OCD, depression, should I go on?

The crazy part is, I've held onto this saying so many times. Let your faith be bigger than your fear. Yet, as I am staring at a magnet on the fridge with this saying, and after almost four years of struggling, I see it. I see it as if it's written down in front of me. Let your God be bigger than your fear.

You see, it can be easy to forget that our faith isn't just regular faith, instead, it's faith in God. This faith is not in what we can do, but in what we know that He can do. Solely relying on faith in ourselves will never work, because we will always fall short. Let's face it, we are human. We have doubts, we waiver at times, and we fall at times. Yet God, He never falls short, never waivers, and He always catches us when we fall. If we choose to rely on something in our own hands, we will always come up

Fear no more

short, yet in God's hands, He always has us. Our faith always matters, and choosing to rest that faith in Jesus Christ is what will move that mountain standing in front of you.

I remember when all this started. I thought that my eyes were on God, however, when I went to leave my house I would constantly tell myself, "I can do this, I can do this." The fact is, I couldn't, but WE could. Me AND God. With God by my side, I can get through this, NEVER in my own strength. There have been times when I have had all the faith in the world to step out, yet fell flat on my face afraid. So, why is that? Why when I would step out having so much strength and faith, come to the threshold of my door, unable to move? This happened because I was putting so much emphasis on the fact that I can do this, that my focus was on the wrong thing, myself. What I needed to focus on was the fact that God can do this through me. And TOGETHER we will get through this.

We need to let our faith in God be bigger than the fears. He is the only One who can truly heal us from the inside out.

Another thing that I want to point out is this. Let your faith be bigger than YOUR fears.

Fear no more

I have come a long way since this all started, and one of the many things that I have learned along the way is this.

Don't claim fear as if it's a possession that you own.

Saying the words my fear, my anxiety, I'm too afraid, etc, is claiming possession of that said fear. It's not mine and I don't want it. God never intended for us to have this kind of fear. God never gave us the spirit of fear, instead, He gave us power, love, and a sound mind.

For God has not given us a spirit of fear, but of power and of love and of a sound mind.

2 Timothy 1:7 NKJV

I want reiterate the fact that our faith matters, and it's where we choose to put our faith that matters the most. The point that I am trying to make is this. Above all else, we need to look to God. After all, this is where our faith truly lies.

Questions

Then said I:

"Ah, Lord God!
Behold, I cannot speak, for I am a youth."

Jeremiah 1:6 NKJV

Fear no more

Just like Jeremiah, I too feel as if I can't speak at times. I struggle with anxiety, agoraphobia, panic attacks, OCD, etc, however, we need to learn that even if we are afraid to do something, we need to push through that fear and rely on God who is stronger, greater, and bigger than that fear. The next time you are afraid to do something that feels scary, ask yourself these questions.

Do you believe that God will protect you while you do it?

Do you believe that there is nothing too hard for God?

Do you trust God more than you trust the fear?

Remember, God is ALWAYS greater than any fear that tries to overtake you.

P.s. In this book you will notice that I don't capitalize the s in satan, or make anything related to him "proper." I actually do this on purpose. Part of the reason we put a capital letter is to highlight and separate names, however, to me it's also a sign of respect, and I have none for him. Therefore, whenever I refer to the enemy I always use a lowercase letter, even if it's the first word in the sentence.

Fear no more

I know that it may sound odd considering we are taught not to do this, but this was intentional. So often we unintentionally give the enemy power in our lives. Through anxiety, fear, depression, or whatever else it is that you are going through. When you come across these "grammar issues," let it be a reminder that satan has no hold on a child of God, and that his lies are not welcome here.

I know that not using a capital letter may bother some, however, I choose to live outside of the box that this world tries to place me in.

Chapter 1
The Beginning

<u>My Journey</u>

I remember the sheer panic when I drove that day. I also remember what followed. Panic, fear, depression, agoraphobia, and a life that felt as if I would always be, broken. It's not that I didn't try to push through the anxiety, because I did, but it never felt like it was enough. Weeks, months, and years went by.

One step forward, ten steps back.

Two steps forward, twenty steps back.

This seemed to be the pattern in my life.

You push, only to fall; you persevere, only to doubt; and you try, only to fail.

However, if you choose to look at life from a different perspective —God's perspective — then you will see that it's all done by design, not pure luck or random choosing, but with purpose. God's purpose.

Fear no more

<u>Wait, what?</u>

So you mean to tell me that my pain was given to me on purpose?

No. I am telling you that your pain was gifted to you, for a purpose.

A woman, when she is in labor, has sorrow because her hour has come; but as soon as she has given birth to the child, she no longer remembers the anguish, for joy that a human being has been born into the world.

John 16:21 NKJV

Out of your pain and out of the laboring, something beautiful will be birthed.

To understand this, you need to look at God's character. Our God is a God of love, and He is a God of purpose. He doesn't want to see you in pain, He wants to see you grow, He doesn't want to see you fail, He wants to see you succeed, and not only to see you succeed, but to walk you through that success.

As a woman who labors hurts for a little while, soon the anguish of her mind and body will be no more. Out of

10

the pain will come purpose. A purpose for her pain, and her pain she will remember no more.

So, what's my story?

How do I know what it feels like to be anxious? How do I know what it's like to have pure panic with every little thing you do? How do I know how you feel? Simply because, I have been through it.

And I am still fighting my way through it.

Over four years later I am still healing, still fighting, and still persevering, in God's strength of course.

I understand

I may not understand exactly what you are going through, but I do understand what it's like. I also know that it's hard. It's hard to break strongholds, hard to keep moving, hard to push, hard to navigate relatives while dealing with this, and overall just hard. My hope is that this book will help you by sharing some of the things that I have learned along the way, as well as some things that I feel God wants me to add to this book.

To God be the glory forever and ever. Amen.

Fear no more

Chapter 2
Not an overnight cure

<u>Miracles</u>

I believe in miracles, and I believe that God can and does heal people in an instant. We serve a God of miracles, and I truly believe that this is more than possible.

But Jesus looked at them and said to them, "With men this is impossible, but with God all things are possible."

Matthew 19:26 NKJV

With that said, regarding my journey, it has been far from an instant healing. However, I have found that even in the pain and even in the long process of healing, there is beauty.

When all of this started, if God would have instantly healed me, I wouldn't be where I am today.

Therefore, as painful as this journey has been, I am also grateful for it. I understand why the scriptures tell us to glory in our tribulations.

Fear no more

And not only that, but we also glory in tribulations, knowing that tribulation produces perseverance; and perseverance, character; and character, hope. Now hope does not disappoint, because the love of God has been poured out in our hearts by the Holy Spirit who was given to us.

Romans 5:3-5 NKJV

Wait, so you want me to be happy that I'm hurting?

It's not that I was happy I was hurting, because I begged God and I pleaded with God to take it all away.

But if you were to give me the chance to go back and change the pain that I endured, and still face, I would tell you, "not a chance."

My growth and the closeness that I feel to God came from that pain, and I wouldn't trade it for the world.
I have struggled with more than just my mental health. I have struggled financially, I have struggled with my physical health, and much more. All while dealing with anxiety, agoraphobia, panic attacks, depression, etc. Sometimes my pain was caused by my own doubts and fears, and sometimes others caused it.

Fear no more

However, God only allowed those things to happen because He wanted to see me grow. So whether it was caused by my own doing or caused by someone else's doing, it was all allowed by God, and done with purpose.

When something happens to you, remind yourself that whatever you go through, God has allowed it. And if God has allowed it, then He most surely has a purpose for it. And at that, a good one.

Fear no more

Chapter 3
Ups and downs

Low Point

It seemed as if everything hit me at a really low point in my life, but I've come to realize that God used that pressure to mold me.

Without pressure there would be no diamonds, and without pressure pottery would never be shaped into the beautiful masterpiece that it was meant to be.

Even with all of these ups and downs, I always knew that they would eventually lead me to helping others. That's not to say that I didn't have my moments of doubt, because I did, and I still do at times.

However, it still amazes me that even in those moments of doubt, God always finds me, picks me up, and encourages me to keep going.

Having doubts doesn't mean that you're failing, it just means that you're human. It's not the doubts that make us

Fear no more

fail, it's what we choose to do with those doubts that matter.

<u>Let me explain</u>

Have you ever heard anyone say that this is not a journey for the fainthearted?

I would have to disagree with this.

You see, I look at things differently. I believe that we all have moments when we feel fainthearted. None of us are perfect, and I believe that we all have moments of doubt and moments when we feel less than courageous. If you say that you haven't had moments of doubt, then you are mistaken.

You shouldn't be ashamed to admit that you have had moments of doubt. It's not shameful, it's honest.

Doubt is a tool that the enemy uses to try and hinder us. Therefore, those doubts will always try to show up and tell us things that aren't true, however, it's not the doubts themselves that hinder us. What hinders us is what we choose to do with those doubts. Do those doubts sit there, do you allow them to take root, or do you recycle them into

Fear no more

16

faith, while **also** choosing to keep your eyes on God rather than the doubt?

Your mind, your choice.

For those who believe, through Jesus Christ, we have been given all power over the enemy and his lies. God has also blessed us with free will. This means that you get to choose what you do with the doubt that comes your way.

We are not responsible for the thoughts that pop up in our minds, but we are responsible for the thoughts that stay in our minds.

The enemy may try to get you to think something, but you are the one who is in full control of what happens with that thought. If your thought is fear, you can choose to keep it, or you can choose to reject it and cast it.

Cast all your anxiety on him because he cares for you.

1 Peter 5:7 NIV

The choice is yours.

<u>But it's not so easy, is it?</u>

I have seen firsthand the struggles that come with casting our thoughts. It's not as simple as it sounds, in fact, it's far

Fear no more

from easy. Not only this, but we can't just resist the thought one time and then expect it to never come back again.

We need to resist the enemy and his thoughts daily, hourly, minute by minute, and second by second.

<u>Cast them down</u>

For the weapons of our warfare are not carnal but mighty in God for pulling down strongholds, casting down arguments and every high thing that exalts itself against the knowledge of God, bringing every thought into captivity to the obedience of Christ, and being ready to punish all disobedience when your obedience is fulfilled.

2 Corinthians 10:4-6 NKJV

Here in these scriptures we are told that we need to take our thoughts captive. Not only this, but it tells us where to cast those thoughts. It says that we are to cast them DOWN and pull them DOWN. We are also supposed to bring low the things that try to exalt themselves over and above the knowledge of God. Here's an example. If a thought of fear pops up in my mind, it's going to try to exalt itself above what I know to be true. That *God has not given us a spirit of fear, but of power and of love and of a sound mind.*

Fear no more

2 Timothy 1:7 This means that I can now lower the thought of fear, and cast DOWN and pull DOWN that thought of fear that is trying to exalt itself above the knowledge of God and what we know to be true, that God didn't give us the spirit of fear. We then bring that thought captive to the obedience of Christ. Here's another one in Joshua 1:9-10.

Have I not commanded you? Be strong and of good courage; do not be afraid, nor be dismayed, for the Lord your God is with you wherever you go. Here we see that it says to be strong and of courage, and it also says not to be afraid nor dismayed. For clarification, dismayed means upset, worried, or agitated because of some unwelcome situation or occurrence. God didn't just tell Joshua this, but it says that He <u>COMMANDED</u> him. And not only this, but we see that the reason he is commanded not to be afraid is because God is with him. So again, we can cast DOWN that thought of fear, and exalt the fact that not only did God command us not to be afraid, but He also gave the best reason as to why we shouldn't be afraid. And that reason is because He is with us.

I did a podcast on this specific topic, so if you want to learn more about bringing your thoughts captive, I put the URL below.

https://youtu.be/CJQV0yAP45k

19

Fear no more

Chapter 4
Remember this

When Jesus was tempted in the desert, He didn't just get tempted once and then return to His day. Instead, satan tempted Jesus three times. Therefore, if you are only expecting to get tempted one time, then you are prematurely letting your guard down and leaving yourself open to an attack. The devil preys on that opening, even if it's just a crack. The fact of the matter is, we were given spiritual armor for a reason, and as long as satan is still around on this earth to tempt us, attack us, and lie to us, we should NEVER put that armor or our guards down. We should also be very aware of when satan attacks the most. This can be when we're tired, overworked, frustrated, hungry, etc. These are some of the easiest times to let your guard down, because your out of it in a sense. Therefore, take note of when these moments happen for you, and make sure that you're alert and ALWAYS in your armor. NEVER let your guard down.

Fear no more

I also want to point out that we so often wonder where God is, especially when we have just finished enduring an attack from the enemy. This is why I want you to remember something. Jesus was tempted three times before the angels came and ministered to Him. He didn't get ministered to in-between these attacks, but only after the attacks were finished. Remember that satan was rebuked not once, not twice, but three times. And it was only after satan had departed from where Jesus was that the angels came and ministered to Him, but it took consistent rebuking and steadfastness on Jesus's end.

Silence

In my own life, some of the hardest moments have been when God has been silent. The times when I pleaded with God to help me, to show me the way, and the times when I cried out, only to hear nothing in return. Here's what I have learned about these silent moments.

1. God's not silent because He's mad at me or because I'm doing something wrong.

We have already established that satan is a liar. And as much as he wants you to believe that your pain is because

God is mad at you, or that you must have done something wrong to get the silent treatment, it's simply not true. Now don't get me wrong, there are moments when we stray or sin and God brings us back, and that journey can be pretty painful. However, this isn't always the case. Sometimes we haven't done anything wrong, but instead, we actually did something right.

<u>Let me explain.</u>

When we read about Job, we read that he was blameless and upright.

In the land of Uz there lived a man whose name was Job. This man was blameless and upright; he feared God and shunned evil.

Job 1:1 NKJV

So what happened? If Job was doing what was right, then why did he suffer so much loss? He lost his children, his servants, and his livestock. He even faced scrutiny from his wife and friends. But why? Did he do something wrong? No, in fact he did what was right. So what happened?

What happened was that there was so much more going on behind the scenes. More than what Job was able to see. All

Fear no more

he was able to see was the fact that everything was being ripped away from him, but God saw so much more. Job saw what was happening with his human eyes, but he had no clue what was going on in the spiritual realm between God and satan. And not only this, but God boasted about Job in heaven. God wasn't allowing these things to happen because He was mad at Job, instead, God was actually proud of Job.

Then the Lord said to Satan, "Have you considered my servant Job? There is no one on earth like him; he is blameless and upright, a man who fears God and shuns evil.

Job 1:8 NKJV

After this, satan states his case as to why Job is blameless and upright. Then God allows satan to test Job, as long as he doesn't take his life.

So you see, God wasn't angry with Job. God loved Job and was proud of who he was. Therefore, don't just assume that you did something wrong because you're going through a trial, instead, pray. Ask God if there is something that you are doing wrong, and if so, to bring it to your attention and

Fear no more

help you correct it. And remember, trials aren't always so black and white. They can be caused by various reasons, and they don't always come just because you're doing something wrong. Here is another example when God said that it was without cause.

Then the Lord said to Satan, "Have you considered My servant Job, that there is none like him on the earth, a blameless and upright man, one who fears God and shuns evil? And still he holds fast to his integrity, although you incited Me against him, to destroy him without cause."

Job 2:3 NKJV

2. Silence doesn't mean absent

Another thing that I have come to realize is this. Just because God is silent, doesn't mean that His presence isn't there. It just means simply what it is, He is silent.

I once heard a quote that said this about the silence of God.

The teacher is always silent during the test.

This is so true. When you take a test, the teacher isn't normally allowed to just give you the answers or help you. The test is exactly that, a test. It's there to test the knowledge of what you have already been taught.

24

Fear no more

Therefore, the silence doesn't mean that God isn't there, it's actually the opposite. The silence can simply mean that you are in the middle of the test. The teacher is always there when you take the test right? You don't usually hear the voice of the teacher, but if you choose to lift up your eyes, you will see that the teacher is still in the room. Still there watching and making sure that you respond correctly to what's been put in front of you. Therefore, if you choose to seek, you can still feel God's presence, even in the silence.

3. Read, Worship & Pray

Some of the best things to do while enduring the silence is to read, worship, and pray.

Don't get frustrated in the silence, instead, keep your eyes on Jesus Christ. Praise Him for what He has already done, recall His faithfulness, tell Him how much you love Him regardless of what He does for you, as He has already done more than any of us will ever deserve, spend time with Him in prayer and reading His word, and don't just read to seek answers, read to find more of Him, more of who He is.

Don't waste the waiting with anger, frustration, and doubts, instead, use those moments to find more of Jesus.

Fear no more

4. Yes, God still hears you

Sometimes, when we are facing trials and we feel that God is silent, we wonder if He even hears us. The simple answer is yes, yes He does.

If we take a look at Job, he cried out for many chapters before even hearing a response from God. And just because God didn't respond right away to Job, it didn't mean that He didn't hear him, and it didn't mean that He wasn't thinking about him. God had a plan the whole time, even in the silence. Job had lost so much, and in that loss, God didn't comfort him the way that I am sure most of us in this situation would want to be comforted. Instead of being met by God's comfort in a really difficult time, Job was met with silence and even more trials. His friends blaming him, his wife trying to get him to turn on God, and even physical pain with painful boils. Sometimes we want God to comfort us because we are so hurt, and sometimes God chooses to allow us to stay in that hurt, to stay in those trials.

I have to point something out here. I'm sure satan uses these moments to tell us that God has abandoned us or that God doesn't care, however, he is a liar. First of all, it was

satan who incited God against Job. Second of all, God doesn't allow things to hurt you. God would NEVER allow anything to just simply hurt you, He loves you too much for that. God ALWAYS has a purpose for EVERYTHING. Sometimes we just don't see it through all of the pain, and sometimes we won't see it at all on this side of life. This is why in ALL circumstances we must trust. Trust that His ways, thoughts, and understanding are always far greater and higher than ours will ever be, and that He can be trusted.

5. Sometimes the test is partly to see if you hold fast to His promises

When Job was tested, satan claimed that if God allowed these things to happen, then Job would curse Him.

But now, stretch out Your hand and touch all that he has, and he will surely curse You to Your face!

Job 1:11

If you want to test someone's faith, you must first throw them into the fire. Look at Shadrach, Meshach, and Abednego. The test wasn't full and complete when they denied the king to his face, no, their true test came when

Fear no more

they were about to be thrown into the fire. Things might get intense when someone says I'll kill you if you don't serve me, but things get the most intense when they actually physically bind you up and bring you towards what looks like death. This was the true test. It's a lot easier for someone to hold fast to their faith when it's only words, however, when those words are faced with morality, pain, or trials, this is when those words get put into action. The action to live by that said faith, or to falter.

6. There is always an ending

Sometimes it feels as if the pain will never end, however, this too shall pass. And God, He is walking through this with you until it does, and even after it does. Whether you hear Him or not, it doesn't negate the fact that He's still there, walking beside you EVERY step of the way.

Fear no more

Chapter 5
A Note to Remember

In Job, God was silent. Job was in pain, sad, and going through a lot. But even though God was silent towards Job, God never took His eyes off of him.

God trusted Job to remain faithful to Him, even in turmoil. God allowed the pain for a time. And even in that time, even in that silence, Job was never alone, and neither are you.

Job had many chapters of turmoil. He cried out to God and was met with silence, for a time, until he was not. And when his time of testing was over, God restored, repaired, and gave Job even more than he had lost during that time of trial. And even though Job didn't get everything back that he wanted (referring to his kids), God still restored Job's joy. Something that seemed to be lost for a time.

God may be silent and you may feel unheard, but the truth is God sees you, God hears you, God loves

Fear no more

you, and He is trusting and believing in you to hold fast to your faith in Him. Therefore, never give up, and never lay down a promise that God has given you. It will come to pass. Wait for it. It will surely come.

Do you believe it?

Chapter 6
Unbelief

While He was still speaking, some came from the ruler of the synagogue's house who said, "Your daughter is dead. Why trouble the Teacher any further?"
As soon as Jesus heard the word that was spoken, He said to the ruler of the synagogue, "Do not be afraid; only believe."

Mark 5:35-36 NKJV

Here we see that as soon as someone spoke a word of unbelief to Jarius, Jesus shut them down. Jesus did this by trying to gain Jarius's focus. Jesus wanted his focus to be on what He was saying about the situation, not on what others were saying. Jesus didn't wait for the doubt to creep into Jarius, instead, He immediately called out to him and comforted him.

As soon as Jesus heard the word that was spoken

We can learn a lot from this. Many times we are in so much

distress, that the pain and doubt block what Jesus is trying to tell us. Here we see Jarius who was concerned for his daughter. She was on the brink of death, and has now just been told that she's dead. And just like you, Jarius had a choice to make. He could choose to believe what things looked like and what he's been told, or he could believe the words of Jesus.

"Do not be afraid; only believe."

Jarius could have chosen to weep. He could have chosen to believe and accept what things looked like. He could have walked away from Jesus when they told him to, however, he chose to listen and believe the words of Jesus instead.

"Do not be afraid; only believe."

His ears were open to what Jesus was telling him in that moment of despair. It's the same thing that I believe Jesus is trying to tell you.

"Do not be afraid; only believe."

Think about it. These people had just come from where his daughter was, therefore, it would be easy to believe that she was indeed gone forever. However, Jarius allowed God's voice to be superior to the voices that surrounded him.

Fear no more

When circumstances leave you breathless and wanting to doubt....DON'T! If Jarius had chosen to doubt Jesus and walk away, he most likely would have never seen the miracle. What we at times fail to realize, is that our faith also affects those around us. If Jarius had chosen to lay down his faith and stop believing for the healing, in turn, his daughter may have never seen the healing either. What you need to realize is that God has plans for you. If you choose to give up now, then your actions affect more than just yourself, and this is a clear example of that. I want to share something that I wrote in my notes the other day. I want you to see that I too have times when I feel like giving up, however, God always find me in my mess and aligns my thoughts with His. We must choose to seek God's voice above the rest, and yes, even above our own.

My note plus some added scriptures and notes

I want to give up, but that's not an excuse to give up. It's just a realization that I need to push harder, that I need to keep going. My life for many. Just as when Jesus was in the Garden of Gethsemane, He didn't quit, He prayed harder. He prayed more fervently. In the midst of despair, He brought that despair to the Father, and He pushed to

Fear no more

complete the task that was set before Him. He did this for you, for me, and for the love that He has for us. Jesus knew that this was why He was sent here in the first place, and even though it caused Him pain and agony, He wanted the Father's will to be done above all else. Even above all of the pain that He was to endure while doing it.

"Now My soul is troubled, and what shall I say? 'Father, save Me from this hour'? But for this purpose I came to this hour. Father, glorify Your name."
Then a voice came from heaven, saying, "I have both glorified it and will glorify it again."

John 12:27-28 NKJV

Then He said to them, "My soul is exceedingly sorrowful, even to death. Stay here and watch."

Mark 14:34 NKJV

He went a little farther, and fell on the ground, and prayed that if it were possible, the hour might pass from Him. And He said, "Abba, Father, all things are possible for You. Take this cup away from Me; nevertheless, not what I will, but what You will."

Mark 14:35-36 NKJV

Fear no more

Jesus was in so much distress that He sweat drops of blood. Even through all of this, Jesus didn't give up, and neither can I. The Father glorified His name through Jesus Christ, and He will again glorify His name through me. I have people that Jesus wants me to help, places He wants me to go, and love that He wants me to share. How selfish if I give up before it was all completed.

This life that God has given me, it's not about me. It's bigger than me. And I intend to finish the race that He has set before me, even though it really hurts sometimes.

All for His glory!

Chapter four

In chapter four I talked about how satan looks for an opening to attack you. This moment in Jarius's life could have been that opening, however, he chose to believe the truth instead of the lie. This reminds me of when Jesus was tempted in the wilderness by satan. We are told that after satan finished tempting Jesus, he departed from Him until an opportune time.

Now when the devil had ended every temptation, he departed from Him until an opportune time.

Luke 4:13 NKJV

Fear no more

When we are hurting either physically or mentally, the devil takes this as an opening, as an opportune time. Think of it this way. Would a lion rather kill a healthy and on the top of its game gazelle, or a gazelle that's limping and injured? It would obviously target and attack the easier prey. The limping gazelle is much easier to catch. Therefore, strengthen your feeble hands and knees, and be strong in the Lord. Stand up straight, firm, and steadfast.

And be sure to do as Jarius did in a moment when circumstances seemed to shift. A moment that LOOKED like the miracle would never happen. He chose to keep his ears open to the words of Jesus, and he not only heard the words, but he believed them.

"Do not be afraid; only believe."

Fear no more

Chapter 7
Crucial points

<u>Stop trying to bear all the weight.</u>

Don't worry about changing yourself. It's not your job to change yourself.

It's our job to do the resisting, and the Holy Spirit's job to do the renewing.

If you focus on being the one to renew your mind, then you will quickly realize that it's too large of a task for you to take on. However, when you choose to focus on God, read His word, praise Him, pray to Him, follow His word, etc, then the change you are seeking will come in time. Remember, our job is to focus on God and let Him do the rest.

We weren't meant to bear the weight of the world on our shoulders, we were meant to conquer the world through Jesus Christ.

Fear no more

No, in all these things we are more than conquerors through him who loved us.

Romans 8:37 NIV

<u>Focus on the good</u>

Focus on the good, and trust God to strengthen you in the process.

Finally, brothers and sisters, whatever is true, whatever is noble, whatever is right, whatever is pure, whatever is lovely, whatever is admirable—if anything is excellent or praiseworthy—think about such things.

Philippians 4:8 NIV

As I said earlier, it's not enough to just resist the negative thoughts once and then be done. If we truly believe that, then we are only setting ourselves up for failure. The truth is, we need to fight. Fight against the thoughts and ways of this world, against principalities and darkness, and fight to live a life for and through Jesus Christ. A life with our minds and thoughts set on God, and not on the things of this world.

For the rest of our lives here on earth, we need to fight together with God, and against the enemy.

38

Fear no more

Set your minds on things above, not on earthly things.

Colossians 3:2 NIV

<u>If only.</u>

It can be easy to say the words, "If only." If only I had my own home, if only this anxiety would go away, if only I had money, if only I had a better job, if only. This is why putting our happiness in the things of this world is so frivolous. There's nothing that can truly satisfy us more than God. Not money, not houses, not a job, and not even the healing that you're asking for. Literally nothing compares to having fellowship with Jesus Christ. Nothing compares to knowing that the Father loves you, to knowing Who's Spirit lives inside of you. Knowing God is everything. Remember that He lasts forever, the treasures of this world don't. And where your treasures lies, there your heart will be also.

Now why do I mention all of this? I want you to see that our focus can be so easily shifted to our wants and needs, when only One thing truly matters. When we focus on what truly matters, the rest seems to fade away. Sometimes slowly, but it most surely does. This is why it's so important not to use the words if only. If only I wasn't

39

afraid, if only I wasn't so sad all the time, etc. Doing this places your focus on the things of this world, rather than on God. The focus should be on learning to be content with what we already have, God. He is more than enough. And when you learn to be content in Him alone, then you learn to be content no matter where you are or what you face in this life. Now I didn't say that it would be easy, because it's far from it. However, it is possible. It's possible to learn contentment even in the midst of adversity, however, you must train to do so. The training happens every time you face an obstacle, and you choose to focus on Jesus instead of that said obstacle. I can attest to the fact that when you first start off it's extremely difficult. You may even feel that you fall more times than you don't. However, the more you keep doing this, the more you build that muscle, and the more you learn to truly be content in Christ alone.

It's not the situations and the circumstances that define us, it's the response to that said situation and circumstance that truly shape who we are.

Fear no more

Chapter 8
The wait

All things take time.

I know that you may be tired of hearing the words, in due time, it takes time, give it time, etc, but the truth is all things really do take time. And I can attest to the fact that sometimes the wait can be the hardest part. I have come to realize that a lot of the times, the best things in life take the most time. Look at the time that it takes from conception to the birth of a child, the time that it takes to grow up to an adult, the time that it takes to learn God's word, and the time that it takes for us to be absent from the body and in heaven with Jesus. All things that are worth waiting for take time. I heard a saying once that said this, "Nature doesn't rush things, yet everything is accomplished." God already has a plan to move you from here to there, and in time, God's time, it will be accomplished. If you try to rush things, it won't speed up the process, but it can actually extend the process. Therefore, don't try to rush things.

Fear no more

One of the things that God has taught me through this process of healing is patience. Your job is to keep your eyes on Him, stop trying to rush things, and trust Him through the process, even when it hurts. Trying to grab the wheel away from God and turning too soon, is like saying that you don't trust Him to drive. Rest assured, God knows exactly where He is taking you far better than you ever will. And not only this, but only God truly knows the why and the way. Remember, only God knows the beginning to the end.

except that no one can find out the work that God does from beginning to end.

Ecclesiastes 3:11

There is a time for everything, and a season for every activity under the heavens: a time to be born and a time to die, a time to plant and a time to uproot, a time to kill and a time to heal, a time to tear down and a time to build, a time to weep and a time to laugh, a time to mourn and a time to dance, a time to scatter stones and a time to gather them, a time to embrace and a time to refrain from embracing, a time to search and a time to give up, a time to keep and a time to throw away, a time to tear and a time to mend, a

Fear no more

time to be silent and a time to speak, a time to love and a time to hate, a time for war and a time for peace.

Ecclesiastes 3:1-8 NIV

Frustrated in the waiting

I know how frustrating the wait can be, however, I can tell you that God has a reason for the wait far beyond what you can see.

God sees everything in its entirety, therefore, God knows what's up ahead, what He wants you to avoid, what He is waiting on, who He is waiting on, what He is preparing you for, etc.

I know how hard waiting can be, but I want you to take a second and realize something. God has not forgotten you.

Are not five sparrows sold for two copper coins? And not one of them is forgotten before God. But the very hairs of your head are all numbered. Do not fear therefore; you are of more value than many sparrows.

Luke 12:6–7 NKJV

Fear no more

You are not forgotten.

God has never, nor will He ever forget about you. If you are waiting, then He has you waiting with purpose and for a purpose. To God you are valuable, and He will never forget about you, even though at times it may feel like He has.

Can a mother forget the baby at her breast and have no compassion on the child she has borne? Though she may forget, I will not forget you! See, I have engraved you on the palms of my hands; your walls are ever before me.

Isaiah 49:15–16 NIV

You are a part of God and God is a part of you. Could your head ever forget about your body? Therefore, He will never forget about you!

Trust that our God is faithful, and He will complete the work that He began in you.

being confident of this, that he who began a good work in you will carry it on to completion until the day of Christ Jesus.

Philippians 1:6 NIV

Fear no more

Trust in the One who loves you enough to make you, the One who engraved you on the palms of His hands, the One who has numbered the hairs on your head, the One who's thoughts for you outnumber the grains of sand, the One who sees your pain, the One who has a plan for that pain, and the One who loves you more than you will ever realize. So much so, that He gave His life as a ransom for yours.

For even the Son of Man did not come to be served, but to serve, and to give his life as a ransom for many."

Mark 10:45 NIV

Fear no more

Chapter 9
Feelings

One of the things that I have come to learn is this, feelings lie. One second we're happy, the next we're crying, one second we're crying, and the next we're yelling. This is why it's so crucial not to go by your feelings. There is a saying that I once heard and it's this, "Feelings are the enemy to obedience to God." This is true in so many ways. I bet that there are a lot of people who have strayed from their calling or where God wanted them because their feelings got in the way. And how many times do we say, I don't <u>feel</u> like it, I <u>feel</u> sad, I <u>feel</u> upset, I <u>feel</u> inadequate, I <u>feel</u> like no one cares about me, <u>I feel I feel I feel</u>. Again, feelings lie. We must learn to separate truth from feelings. God is with me, therefore, even if I don't feel like it, I can do it, I feel sad and upset, but I know that God will carry me through, so I will focus on Him instead of the pain, I feel inadequate, but I don't need to be adequate, because God is more than enough, and where I lack God more than

Fear no more

makes up for, and when I am weak, God is my strength, I feel alone, yet I know in God's word He assures me that I am never alone, and that He would never leave me nor forsake me. As I said, we must learn to separate lies from truths. And remember, never go solely by your feelings, because they lie. This is one of the many reasons why it's so crucial to read your Bible, however, we will get to that later.

Remember that your heart isn't always correct, but God is, therefore, look to Him above the noise and above all else, for only He truly knows all things.

For if our heart condemns us, God is greater than our heart, and knows all things.

1 John 3:20

Fear no more

Chapter 10
God cares

Have you ever wondered if God even cares about what you are going through? If so, here is your answer.

God cares about you so much more than you know. You're not a passing thought in His mind, but a steady one.

How precious also are Your thoughts to me, O God! How great is the sum of them! If I should count them, they would be more in number than the sand; When I awake, I am still with You.

Psalms 139:17-18 NKJV

You are so precious to God. Don't believe for one second that He doesn't care. If you do, you are believing a lie from the enemy that says you don't matter. God loves you far beyond any words that I could ever express to you. And if you truly didn't matter to God, if He truly didn't care about you, then why would He have gone through so much pain and suffering to save you?

Fear no more

Has God abandoned me?

Never.

If God hasn't abandoned me, then why won't He help me?

Sometimes our version of helping is different from God's, however, I can tell you this.

Sometimes God needs to break something down first, before building something better.

As I said earlier, "When all of this started, if God had instantly healed me, I wouldn't be where I am today."

The breaking down is what made me where I am, and who I am today.

God needed to remove the things that didn't belong in me, so that He could replace it with something better. More of Himself.

Let's say that I want to build a house. I go in my backyard and grab some sand, then I start building. If one day I decide that I want to make my house sturdier, what would I have to do? I couldn't just lay bricks on top of the sand could I? I would need to tear it down first. If I try to build

on top of what's already there, the house would fall. Why? Because the foundation isn't built correctly. I need something firmer than mere sand to build upon. I would first need to remove all of that sand, in order to rebuild something better, something stronger, and something that can withstand the storms of this life.

We have to be built on the Cornerstone, that is, Jesus Christ. If we build upon anything else, then the fall of that house will be great.

"Therefore whoever hears these sayings of Mine, and does them, I will liken him to a wise man who built his house on the rock: and the rain descended, the floods came, and the winds blew and beat on that house; and it did not fall, for it was founded on the rock.

"But everyone who hears these sayings of Mine, and does not do them, will be like a foolish man who built his house on the sand: and the rain descended, the floods came, and the winds blew and beat on that house; and it fell. And great was its fall."

Matthew 7:24-27 NKJV

Fear no more

Therefore, if you choose to build on anything else aside from Jesus Christ, then you are building on sand, and your building will fall.

Remember, sometimes God will allow certain trials in our lives to remove the things that don't belong. And if you ever wonder if God is even helping you, remember that He is. He is helping you even when it hurts, even when it doesn't look like it, and even when you don't feel like He is. Remember what I said in the beginning of this chapter, "Sometimes our version of helping is different from God's."

God is helping you, it's just hard to see right now. But in time, you will.

According to the grace of God which was given to me, as a wise master builder I have laid the foundation, and another builds on it. But let each one take heed how he builds on it. For no other foundation can anyone lay than that which is laid, which is Jesus Christ. Now if anyone builds on this foundation with gold, silver, precious stones, wood, hay, straw, each one's work will become clear; for the Day will declare it, because it will be revealed by fire; and the fire will test each one's work, of what sort it is. If anyone's work

Fear no more

which he has built on it endures, he will receive a reward. If anyone's work is burned, he will suffer loss; but he himself will be saved, yet so as through fire.

1 Corinthians 3:10-15 NKJV

Fear no more

Chapter 11
Never alone

♡

<u>Remember this</u>

Always remember that you are never alone. God is walking through this with you.

Eventually, you will be led to the other side of what you are facing, and you will be amazed at all of the beauty that came from the pain.

In moments when we feel alone and abandoned, we must remember what God has said. God will NEVER leave us nor forsake us.

For He Himself has said, "I will never leave you nor forsake you."

Hebrews 13:5

I know how hard it can be when facing various trials. You may feel forgotten, overwhelmed, and alone. As I am writing this my thoughts are brought to Jesus. He knew

that His sheep would scatter, and He knew that it would look as if He was alone, yet what He ultimately knew superseded what things looked like.

Indeed the hour is coming, yes, has now come, that you will be scattered, each to his own, and will leave Me alone. And yet I am not alone, because the Father is with Me. These things I have spoken to you, that in Me you may have peace. In the world you will have tribulation; but be of good cheer, I have overcome the world."

John 16:32-33 NKJV

Jesus knew that it would look like He was alone, yet He also knew the truth. That just because something looked true, didn't make is so. And to push this even further, Jesus knew well before this moment even happened that it would look as if He was alone. We see this in the above scripture as well as others. As an example, we see this in Zechariah 13:7, Mark 14:27, and also in Matthew 26:31.

Then Jesus told them, "This very night you will all fall away on account of me, for it is written:
" 'I will strike the shepherd,
and the sheep of the flock will be scattered.'

Matthew 26:31 NIV

Jesus knew what was to come. Jesus knew that it would look like He was alone, and it would look as if He was abandoned, yet He also knew that He wasn't. You can remember this too. That there may be times in your life when you too feel alone, and it looks like you have been abandoned by everyone and everything. Yet, in all this, know that you too are NEVER alone. And just as Jesus overcame this world, you too have the power to do so as well, for He is in you, and you in Him.

You are of God, little children, and have overcome them, because He who is in you is greater than he who is in the world.

1 John 4:4 NKJV

In Psalm 139 we are reminded that God is always with us, no matter where we are.

O Lord, You have searched me and known me.
You know my sitting down and my rising up;
You understand my thought afar off.
You comprehend my path and my lying down,
And are acquainted with all my ways.
For there is not a word on my tongue,
But behold, O Lord, You know it altogether.

Fear no more

You have hedged me behind and before,
And laid Your hand upon me.
Such knowledge is too wonderful for me;
It is high, I cannot attain it.
Where can I go from Your Spirit?
Or where can I flee from Your presence?
If I ascend into heaven, You are there;
If I make my bed in hell, behold, You are there.
If I take the wings of the morning,
And dwell in the uttermost parts of the sea,
Even there Your hand shall lead me,
And Your right hand shall hold me.
If I say, "Surely the darkness shall fall on me,"
Even the night shall be light about me;
Indeed, the darkness shall not hide from You,
But the night shines as the day;
The darkness and the light are both alike to You.
For You formed my inward parts;
You covered me in my mother's womb.
I will praise You, for I am fearfully and wonderfully made;
Marvelous are Your works,
And that my soul knows very well.
My frame was not hidden from You,

Fear no more

These verses show us that even if you feel lost, God knows EXACTLY where you are. When you sit, when you rise, when you're scared, and when you're unsure. Whatever you are feeling in this moment, even if you feel you are in the darkest valley, God sees you all the same. For even the darkness can not escape God's light. Think about it this way. If I am in a pitch black room and I turn on a light, what happens? That darkness has no choice but to flee. God meant it when He said that darkness can't overcome light. We even see this here on earth with our own eyes. I believe

Fear no more

that God did this on purpose, at least in part to show us how light overcomes darkness. And to give another example, the moon gives light and allows us to see, even when it's dark.

Therefore, remember that while there may be darkness, there is always a Light to overcome it.

The light shines in the darkness, and the darkness has not overcome it.

John 1:5 NIV

The Light that shines when you feel like all you see is darkness is Jesus Christ. There is no light purer, truer, or brighter than He.

That was the true Light which gives light to every man coming into the world.

John 1:9 NKJV

Then Jesus spoke to them again, saying, "I am the light of the world. He who follows Me shall not walk in darkness, but have the light of life."

John 8:12 NKJV

Fear no more

Even when you can't see things clearly, and even when all you see is darkness, remember that God still knows the way regardless.

I am reminded in these moments of a scripture in 1 Kings.

The Lord said, "Go out and stand on the mountain in the presence of the Lord, for the Lord is about to pass by." Then a great and powerful wind tore the mountains apart and shattered the rocks before the Lord, but the Lord was not in the wind. After the wind there was an earthquake, but the Lord was not in the earthquake. After the earthquake came a fire, but the Lord was not in the fire. And after the fire came a gentle whisper. When Elijah heard it, he pulled his cloak over his face and went out and stood at the mouth of the cave.
Then a voice said to him, "What are you doing here, Elijah?"

1 Kings 19:11-13 NIV

If you notice, God called Elijah to go out. And before God revealed why He had called Him, He was faced with wind that tore the mountains apart and shattered the rocks, there was an earthquake, and then there was fire. God has also

called you. Right now you are most likely in that wind, earthquake, and fire. However, it wasn't until after these things came to pass, that God spoke to Elijah to reveal why He had called him to stand on the mountain.

You may not realize it now, but that wind, earthquake, and fire, could be getting you prepared to hear what God has to say to you next. Don't become so focused on that earthquake, that you forget Who is standing there watching over you until it passes.

Elijah saw the storm, and Elijah may have even felt the storm, but God didn't. This is a perfect reminder that when we are in a storm, it may feel large and uncertain, and you may be unable to see your way out, but God has a clear view. When all you see is debris, God sees perfectly the way to go. God is not moved by life's circumstances. He is God, and He already knows the outcome beforehand. He knows the ending before we even see the beginning.

I also want you to notice what came after all of these loud and destructive noises. What came after was a small still voice. A gentle whisper. Sometimes we look for this grand sign and a loud voice, however, sometimes God chooses to be a whisper. Therefore, if we don't pay close attention we

may miss it, because we are only looking for something loud. When we are only looking for a loud voice, we can unintentionally disregard the small still voice. I also did a short podcast episode on this subject if you want to hear more. I will place the URL below.

https://youtu.be/FQoXe8Dzpb4

Remember, whenever you feel overwhelmed and unsure of the way to go, look to the only One who knows the way out. Look to God, be still in His presence, and know that He already knows the way to go. And even when you don't know the way, He never loses sight of it. God has everything figured out. Be patient and trust Him.

When my spirit was overwhelmed within me,
Then You knew my path.

Psalm 142:3 NKJV

Remember, if you can't see clearly, don't try to look for the way out. Instead, look to God and He will lead you there.

God will never leave your side, and He's guiding you even when you don't see it. Trust Him.

Fear no more

Oh what a loving God we have. His love for us stretches across oceans, crosses valleys, scales mountains, and finds us wherever we may be.

The Lord will guide you always

Isaiah 58:11 NIV

Don't lose hope.

I would have lost heart, unless I had believed That I would see the goodness of the LORD In the land of the living. Wait on the LORD; Be of good courage, And He shall strengthen your heart; Wait, I say, on the LORD!

Psalms 27:13–14 NKJV

The definition of hope is this.

a feeling of expectation and desire for a certain thing to happen.

This means that we don't hope for what we already have or see, we hope for what we don't have and what we can't see. The best way to explain this is found in Romans.

For in this hope we were saved. But hope that is seen is no hope at all. Who hopes for what they already have? But if we hope for what we do not yet have, we wait for it patiently.

Romans 8:24-25 NIV

Fear no more

It's easy to lose hope when everything around you feels like it's crumbling, however, I must urge you to hold on. You must remember that the reason for your hope remains in One who is trustworthy, Jesus Christ. So often we lose hope because we forget the One who holds that said hope.

We feel like things aren't working out, things aren't changing, and that breakthrough looks like it will never happen. It's in these moments that we must QUICKLY remember that the hope we have isn't just empty hope, but filled with the love of Jesus Christ. Therefore, if we give up on the hope within us, then we are ultimately giving up on Jesus Christ. I know how this may sound, so let me explain

Let's read this scripture below for an example.

And we know that all things work together for good to those who love God, to those who are the called according to His purpose.

Romans 8:28

Here we see that if you are a follower of Christ, then God works all things <u>together</u> for good. This doesn't mean that all things will always be good, instead, it means that all things, even the bad things, will be worked <u>together</u> for good.

Sometimes it takes that wilderness journey to appreciate more the land flowing with milk and honey.

This scripture says that He will work all things together for good, and this is a promise. God promises us that all things in our life, even those things that hurt us, will be worked together to produce something good. Therefore, if you choose in the middle of a trial to give up, say that God has abandoned you, and turn away from thinking that anything good will come of the situation, then you are essentially questioning the faithfulness of God. You are ultimately giving up on what God tells you that He will do. And God tells us through Paul that He will work it out for good, so we must believe Him, regardless of how we feel or how things look. Yes, even when it hurts, even when it's painful, and even when we feel like giving up, we must not.

And remember, if we doubt God's promises, then we are in turn choosing to doubt God's character as well.

If we say that we trust God, we must follow our words through with action, even when we feel like giving up. Don't lose your hope, and remember Who holds that said hope. Keep fighting and keep persevering. The end result will be more than worth it!

Fear no more

Chapter 13
what if I mess up?

I think that a common misconception is that we will never mess up. Of course we will mess up at times! Jesus died for us because we weren't perfect. We couldn't possibly follow God's law without any mistakes, no matter how hard we tried. Therefore, when you ask the question, "What if I mess up?", my response is simple. That's where grace comes in.

Grace is a precious gift from God, and the grace that He gives us will never run out.

The Israelite's didn't believe in what God could do and would do for them. Because of this, they wandered in the wilderness for 40 years. There was a moment recently where I thought this too. That because I had a moment of doubt, would I too miss the blessing that God had for me, all because of my unbelief. This quick thought was met with a reminder. I was reminded of a Key component that they didn't have back then, One that we now have today.

Fear no more

The redemption of Jesus Christ. You see, when the Israelite's doubted, this hadn't happened yet. They were still in their sins, and the sacrifices still needed to be made. Now however, we are no longer under law, but under grace. And there is now therefore no condemnation for those who are in Christ Jesus. I am free from the law of sin and death. This doesn't mean that I will never mess up, but what it does mean is that when I do, I am forgiven. My sins are as far as the east is from the west, meaning that they never meet, and I am no longer held by that past mistake, instead, I am free from it and forgiven. I no longer walk according to the flesh, for I am a new creation in Christ Jesus. One that walks in the Spirit. And even though I mess up at times, God's grace, mercy, and love, are always there to pick me up. For His grace is always sufficient for me, even in my weakness.

But he said to me, "My grace is sufficient for you, for my power is made perfect in weakness." Therefore I will boast all the more gladly about my weaknesses, so that Christ's power may rest on me.

2 Corinthians 12:9

Fear no more

As an example, I used to get really mad at myself when I had a panic attack. I felt so guilty because I didn't trust God in those moments, however, I now understand God's grace. I now understand that when I say I'm sorry, He truly does forgive me. I can then pick myself up and try to do better next time. Therefore, in those moments when you are feeling guilty for messing up, remember this. Guilt was defeated at the cross. When you tell God you're sorry, He doesn't hold it over you, instead, He forgives you. God doesn't give as the world gives, and His forgiveness is true forgiveness. He's not mad at you, He just wants you. He wants you to come to Him, regardless of what you have done. And even though you may have fallen down, He still wants you all the same. He doesn't want to yell at you, He wants to forgive you and hold you through it.

Fear no more

Chapter 14
You are important

One of the many things that I have learned along the way is this. We are all important to the body of Christ. We all matter, we all have a place, and we all need each other.

You and me, we are both important. Not one more than the other. Each member of the body of Christ needs each other, and each member has a certain purpose in the kingdom of God. Not only this, but God doesn't love one more than the other. If you place two people next to each other, and one has been a pastor for 50 years and has brought millions to Jesus, and the other is a Mom of 3 kids who tries her best to raise her kids to follow Jesus, God loves them both the same. One is not more important than the other, one is not loved more than the other, and both are wanted.

Now I say this because I want you to realize your importance. It can be easy to say, "I'm too afraid and God can just use someone else," but guess what? God doesn't want someone else to do the job that He made you for, He

wants you. I also say this because I want you to realize that number one, you need to beat this thing, and number two, God has something planned for you when you do. The enemy will try his best to get you to think that you should just give up, that you should just deal with the anxiety, pain, panic attacks, depression, etc. I know this because I have been there. I used to think that the anxiety, agoraphobia, etc, were a thorn in my side that God wanted there. I couldn't have been farther from the truth. God never wanted me to be afraid. How do I know this? Because His word says so. Why do you think there are so many scriptures that tell us not to be afraid? It's because God knew that this is something we would face, and He wanted us to know that we have nothing to be afraid of, because He is with us.

Therefore, remember that you are important to God and you matter. You matter to God, and you matter to the body of Christ. God has such great plans for you. Don't let those plans pass you by because you decide to give up and allow the enemy to trample you. Remember, we have been given the power to trample the enemy, not the other way around.

Fear no more

Therefore, remember that you are important to God and you matter. You matter to God, and you matter to the body of Christ. God has such great plans for you, don't let those plans pass you by because you decide to give up and allow the enemy to trample you. Remember, we are given the power to trample him, not the other way around.

I have given you authority to trample on snakes and scorpions and to overcome all the power of the enemy; nothing will harm you.

Luke 10:18-20

71

Fear no more

Chapter 15
It's okay

I have come to terms with the fact that it's okay to not be okay. As a matter of fact, right now I can admit that I'm not okay. I started this book when it was over 4 years of living with relatives, but now as I recently felt it on my heart to continue this book, I'm at over 5 years. It has been really hard to say the least. If you don't feel okay either, I want you to know that it's okay to have bad days. We all have bad days. God understands and offers you His grace in return. I wanted to express to you how I feel in this moment, however, I think that a page from my notes would help the most. I'll write that below.

And remember, it's okay to not be okay sometimes. God wants us to come to Him as we are. Whether we're angry, hurt, upset, or sad, He wants us to be honest with Him no matter how we feel.

The note that I'm going to share was written after reading the scripture below in Habakkuk.

Fear no more

I will stand my watch
And set myself on the rampart,
And watch to see what He will say to me,
And what I will answer when I am corrected.

Habakkuk 2:1 NKJV

You see, Habakkuk was asking how long he must cry and God not hear. He was in distress, and although he said these words, he ended it with the scripture above, as if he knew that he would be corrected. Here are my notes below.

Here he makes a statement as if he knew he would be corrected.

When we are in distress we feel forgotten. We feel alone. However, even though at times we may feel this way, deep down we know that it's not true. Not in the least.

Waiting at times can make us feel weak. And it's in that weakness that we question God at times, just like Habakkuk did. He was in distress, asking how long. How long must he cry. He felt unheard by God, however, here's the thing about feelings, they lie. They make you doubt, they make you stray, and they hurt.

They lie because regardless of how forgotten you may feel,

God would never forget about you. You are the work of
His hand, and He loves you.

But now, O Lord,
You are our Father;
We are the clay, and You our potter;
And all we are the work of Your hand.

Isaiah 64:8 NKJV

The Lord has appeared of old to me, saying:
"Yes, I have loved you with an everlasting love;
Therefore with lovingkindness I have drawn you.

Jeremiah 31:3 NKJV

Changing seasons

There is an appointed time for seasons to change. We must
wait for it, for it will surely come. In the meantime, we
must live with our faith, and we must die with our faith.
At the moment of writing this, I too am having a hard time.
I am in great distress. I feel like God has passed me by, yet
I know He is right here with me, and that in His time He
will redeem that which has been lost. I feel forgotten, yet I
know in my heart God would never forget the one He
loves. I feel weak, yet I know in Him I am made strong.

Fear no more

I feel alone, yet I know He is always with me. I feel like giving up, yet I know God's love, grace, and mercy will never let me. I feel angry, yet I feel His love regardless.

Sometimes, we may feel and even say these things, yet the Holy Spirit reminds us of all things. He reminds us of the truth. He reminds us that we are loved, wanted, and that we are going to be okay. No matter how deep the valley, it always leads to a river. A river of grace and love, a river that says come all you who are thirsty, weary, and burdened, and I will give you rest. A river that never stops flowing.

So yes, waiting seasons can be extremely difficult, but if you choose to look close enough, you will see that there is a Light that's guiding you. One that's encouraging you to keep going and not give up.

You have to keep fighting. Don't let there be another option.

I for one won't give up. I know God won't let me. He's just that good of a God!

He has made everything beautiful in its time.

Ecclesiastes 3:11 NKJV

Fear no more

As I have said, it's much easier said than done. So what are some of the things that we can do to fight these negative thoughts? How can we fight anxiety, depression, panic, and agoraphobia?

I want to share some of the things that I have learned along the way, but before I share them with you, I want you to know something.

You are not fighting this alone.

Not only is God with you, but there are other believers around the world who are experiencing things similar to what you face.

You are NEVER alone in your battles.

Be alert and of sober mind. Your enemy the devil prowls around like a roaring lion looking for someone to devour. Resist him, standing firm in the faith, because you know that the family of believers throughout the world is undergoing the same kind of sufferings.

1 Peter 5:8-9 NIV

Fear no more

If I could see all of the tears that I have cried these past 4 years, I would fill an ocean, or a pool at best.

I've had my moments of doubt, and I've struggled with agoraphobia, OCD, anxiety, panic attacks, and depression. I have been in agony over not being able to leave my home, over not feeling strong enough to even step out of my front door. This then grew into me being too afraid to even go in my kitchen. I have had panic attacks, I have felt sad and depressed, and I have had thoughts that tell me that this pain would never end, that I would always be like this. But through all of this, I have seen so much of God's love, mercy, forgiveness, strength, courage, protection, provision, and so much more. I have seen a God who cares, a God who loves, and a God who holds, even though I never deserve any of it.

I have seen God work in my life in mighty ways. I have seen a God who never fails, a God who deserves all of the glory for where I am today, a God who I am so grateful to be able to call mine, and a God who I am privileged and honored to follow all the days of my life and thereafter, regardless of how difficult those days may be. I am so extremely grateful and thankful that He loves me the way that He does.

Fear no more

And as painful as all of this has been, I wouldn't trade it for the world. Because through all of it, I found more of Jesus and less of me.

<u>Where this pain leads</u>

Although I may be unsure of what the future holds for me in this life, one of the things that I do know is where this pain will lead. I do hope for and believe that it will lead to somewhere that will help a lot of people, but I mean beyond that. I see beyond that and into the eternal place that I am running to. When you choose to look past all of the pain of this life, you see more than the everyday struggles. Because in the long run, when all is said and done, and we are spending eternity with a God who loves us so much, these days that we find ourselves in pain, tears, and trials, will be gone. They will be no more.

And God will wipe away every tear from their eyes; there shall be no more death, nor sorrow, nor crying. There shall be no more pain, for the former things have passed away.

Revelation 21:4 NKJV

So yes, I do believe that I will see something beautiful birthed from all of this pain, in this life. But I also see

beyond that and into the eternal. That is truly what we are fighting for, and that is truly what we are running towards.

We are running towards the arms of Jesus.

Fear no more

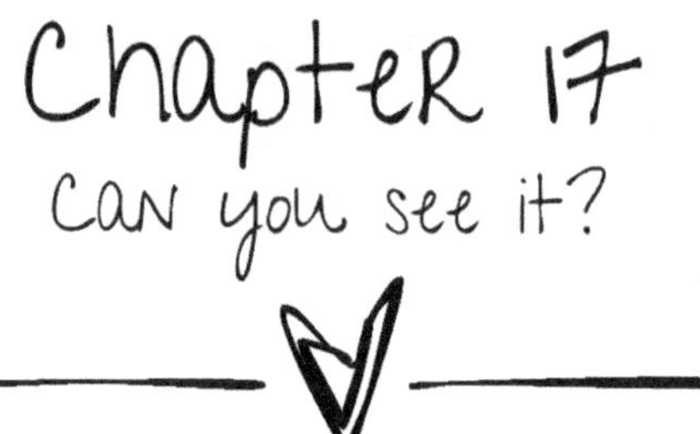

The pain that you feel, the sorrow, and the trials, gone, in an instant.

I still think about this sometimes. The day when we are in constant joy. No crying, no sadness, and no more pain. Living the rest of eternity right by Jesus's side.

Such a beautiful thought, that will one day become a beautiful reality.

<u>The rest is temporary</u>

However, for now I have come to terms with the fact that in this life we will always face adversity.

We have to remember that this life, this world, it's not our home. We are but foreigners here, and this place is only temporary.

We are homesick, longing for something greater than this world. An eternity with Jesus.

For here we do not have an enduring city, but we are looking for the city that is to come.

Hebrews 13:14 NIV

All these people were still living by faith when they died. They did not receive the things promised; they only saw them and welcomed them from a distance, admitting that they were foreigners and strangers on earth. People who say such things show that they are looking for a country of their own. If they had been thinking of the country they had left, they would have had opportunity to return. Instead, they were longing for a better country—a heavenly one. Therefore God is not ashamed to be called their God, for he has prepared a city for them.

Hebrews 11:13-16 NIV

But our citizenship is in heaven. And we eagerly await a Savior from there, the Lord Jesus Christ, who, by the power that enables him to bring everything under his control, will transform our lowly bodies so that they will be like his glorious body.

Philippians 3:20-21 NIV

Fear no more

This world is only a temporary place for us to live, but not where we are meant to be forever.

So although we struggle much in this life, we also find comfort in the fact that it's all temporary. And when we can learn to focus on the eternal, rather than the temporary, we start to realize that this pain won't last forever. Not only should we believe that God will heal us in this life, but we also look forward to what comes after this life, and into the eternal.

Try to remember that as painful as this life can be at times, we have a better, eternal home waiting for us. One unlike any other.

My Father's house has many rooms; if that were not so, would I have told you that I am going there to prepare a place for you?

John 14:2 NIV

Fear no more

Chapter 18
Do you believe?

In Matthew we hear about two men who were blind.

When Jesus departed from there, two blind men followed Him, crying out and saying, "Son of David, have mercy on us!"

And when He had come into the house, the blind men came to Him. And Jesus said to them, "Do you believe that I am able to do this?"

They said to Him, "Yes, Lord."

Then He touched their eyes, saying, "According to your faith let it be to you." And their eyes were opened. And Jesus sternly warned them, saying, "See that no one knows it."

Matthew 9:27-30 NKJV

Do you remember in the beginning of this book when I said that your faith always matters? It really does, and this is a

Fear no more

perfect example of that. You see, our faith works together **with** God. Jesus tells us that we only need a mustard seed of faith to move a mountain. Therefore, I am going to ask you a similar question to what Jesus asked the blind men.

Do you believe that Jesus is able to heal you?

Don't say yes unless you truly mean it. And if you truly mean it, then remember that the healing doesn't always come instantly, I am proof of that. If you answered yes to the first question, then you are faced with another two questions.

Are you willing to wait for it?

And are you willing to trust God in the process?

I want to add that years ago I had a dream. In this dream Jesus showed me that He healed me. In my mind I thought it was instant, and I had faith that it was. However, as the days went on I was still dealing with it, even though I had so much faith that I was healed. It took a long time to actually see what was promised me, and I still deal with these issues even to this day, however, the difference is I can now see the end.

I've come to learn that it's not how far you have left to

Fear no more

go, it's opening your eyes and seeing how far you've already come.

In that waiting I had to hold onto the promise that I was healed. There were days when I was so weak from the anguish, that I even had trouble lifting myself off the floor. I was that weak. However, I still held on. And the days when I felt like I couldn't hold on, God was my strength, and He still is. He offered me grace when I deserved none.

I say all of these things to show you a few points.

1. Don't stop believing for the healing, no matter how long it's been.
2. Your weakness will always be met with God's strength and grace.
3. If God gives you a promise, He will come through. Sometimes it just takes time, however, rest assured that He has His reasons for the wait.
4. Every day that passes is another opportunity for you to declare these words, "Today is the day that I am healed."

I also want to point out that Jesus showed His willingness to heal us multiple times in the Bible. Here's an example.

When He had come down from the mountain, great multitudes followed Him. And behold, a leper came and worshiped Him, saying, "Lord, if You are willing, You can make me clean."

Then Jesus put out His hand and touched him, saying, "I am willing; be cleansed." Immediately his leprosy was cleansed.

Matthew 8:1-3

If Jesus hasn't healed you yet, it doesn't mean that He's not willing, it just means that He has a different plan than you.

Now as Jesus passed by, He saw a man who was blind from birth. And His disciples asked Him, saying, "Rabbi, who sinned, this man or his parents, that he was born blind?" Jesus answered, "Neither this man nor his parents sinned, but that the works of God should be revealed in him.

John 9:1-3

Since the beginning of this journey, I have always declared this fact. I am going to be healed, and I am going to help others going through the same or similar situations.

86

Fear no more

If I have to go through all of this pain, just so I can see someone else helped by that pain, it's worth it.

We are told to take up our cross and follow after Jesus. Jesus laid down His life for many, and I am willing to do the same. Obviously He did way more than I ever could, however, even if I only help one person, my one life is worth the life of that one. Jesus, He always finds the one. The one always matters to Him, and they matter to me too.

Chapter 19
The healing

I want to ask you a question. If you are healed, what are you planning on doing with that healing?

It can be easy once you are healed to go about life as usual. However, I must urge you not to put the healing behind you, but to use if for God's glory.

Now He arose from the synagogue and entered Simon's house. But Simon's wife's mother was sick with a high fever, and they made request of Him concerning her. So He stood over her and rebuked the fever, and it left her. And immediately she arose and served them.

Luke 4:38-39

Here we see that IMMEDIATELY after she was healed, she served. She didn't get healed and then go out and party, she stayed with Jesus and served Him. You too, go and do likewise.

Fear no more

Chapter 20
Adversity

Have you ever been afraid to tell someone about the issues you face? Maybe you fear that they will judge you, not understand you, or think that you are less than. I won't sugar coat the fact that you may encounter this.

However, don't let someone else's actions prevent you from seeking wise counsel.

The truth is, there will always be someone who doesn't understand you, someone who criticizes you, or someone who makes you feel less than. Therefore, if you are trying to seek wise counsel, ask God to place someone on your path that can give you **sound** Biblical advice. If you are wondering if someone is giving you wise counsel, ask God. Stack what they are saying and compare it to God's word, also look at the life that they live. Sometimes, simply looking at how someone lives, can be a great indicator of if their advice has the potential to be unwise.

Fear no more

Don't let someone's bad actions deter you from asking for help. It's possible that person was placed there by the enemy to deter you from the next person that you were going to ask. The one who was going to give you wise counsel.

The world's standard

I guess that's the world's standard now. To say that if you are a Christian, then you shouldn't struggle.

One time I was in a church Bible study. We were sitting around a table and someone was voicing their struggles? Do you know what the people around the table responded with? They said that basically if they are going through something, it's because of something that they have done. It was like a total Job's friends moment. Assuming that because you are suffering, it's because of something you did. It was more than one person who agreed with the statement. As they were ganging up on this person, one lady even said something along the lines of, "I haven't struggled in a long time." She said this with a proud look on her face, as if because she didn't struggle, she was more of a Christian than someone struggling. However, this

Fear no more

advice was that of the world, and not of God. Remember that they persecuted Jesus, and they will persecute you too.

If the world hates you, keep in mind that it hated me first. If you belonged to the world, it would love you as its own. As it is, you do not belong to the world, but I have chosen you out of the world. That is why the world hates you. Remember what I told you: 'A servant is not greater than his master.' If they persecuted me, they will persecute you also. If they obeyed my teaching, they will obey yours also. They will treat you this way because of my name, for they do not know the one who sent me.

John 15:18-21

Now this isn't to say that they didn't believe or follow Jesus. What I am saying is that the advice that they gave was that of the worlds, and not of God. And remember that just because someone is a follower of Jesus, it doesn't mean that everything they say is correct.

Then Peter took Him aside and began to rebuke Him, saying, "Far be it from You, Lord; this shall not happen to You!"

But He turned and said to Peter, "Get behind Me, Satan!

Fear no more

You are an offense to Me, for you are not mindful of the things of God, but the things of men."

Matthew 16:22-23 NKJV

<u>Let me make something clear.</u>

Don't ever let anyone make you believe that if you are a Christian you shouldn't struggle.

Why? Because it's not a true statement. Throughout the scriptures we read about many people who struggled with the narrow path. I mean, it's called the narrow path for a reason. If it were easy, wouldn't more people find it?

Enter through the narrow gate. For wide is the gate and broad is the road that leads to destruction, and many enter through it. But small is the gate and narrow the road that leads to life, and only a few find it.

Matthew 7:13-14 NIV

With that said, I also want to add this.

Don't hold a grudge against those who have mistreated you.

Instead, pray for them. I know, it's easier said than done. However, holding a grudge against others doesn't affect

92

Fear no more

them, it affects you.

And whether it's someone who isn't being there for you in one of the hardest times of your life, or someone who has mistreated you, you should still forgive them.

How do we actually follow this commandment when it's just so hard?

"You have heard that it was said, 'Love your neighbor and hate your enemy.' But I tell you, love your enemies and pray for those who persecute you, that you may be children of your Father in heaven. He causes his sun to rise on the evil and the good, and sends rain on the righteous and the unrighteous. If you love those who love you, what reward will you get? Are not even the tax collectors doing that? And if you greet only your own people, what are you doing more than others? Do not even pagans do that? Be perfect, therefore, as your heavenly Father is perfect.

Matthew 5:43–48 NIV

How easy it would be to just hate those who hate you, or to mistreat those who mistreat you. But the thing is, we weren't called for easy. We were called to follow the narrow path. In these moments, try to remember the words

that Jesus said when they were persecuting Him.

Then Jesus said, "Father, forgive them, for they do not know what they do."

Luke 23:34 NKJV

What does this have to do with anxiety?

It has a lot to do with it actually. When you choose to hold onto bitterness, anger, resentment, etc, it puts a damper on your growth. Do you remember when I said "Holding a grudge against others doesn't affect them, it affects you?" When I said that, I meant it.

There are some things that you can't bring with you where God is taking you. Unforgiveness is one of them. Whatever anyone else has done, and even what you have done, you have to let it go.

In order to move forward, God is going to ask us to leave some things behind.

If you can't let go of your past, you will have trouble seeing your future.

I want to share a dream that I had over a year ago. There was a water slide and my husband and two of my kids

started climbing up. I wasn't going to go at first, but I decided to even though I was scared. I stopped before getting to the bottom of the slide because I saw a sign. The sign said that it was deep. This made me afraid. I saw my husband swim to the deep bottom because he was waiting for me. He did this so he could watch over me in case I needed help. I tried to get off the slide before it hit the deep waters. I got off by going on the side of the slide, and I tried to swim towards the shore, but there was a strong current that wouldn't let me swim backwards. I then went back on the slide and looked at the lifeguard that was there. I asked her this question, "How do I swim against the current?" She answered me, "You can't." After I woke up I wrote down these words.

I can't go backwards. I have to go forward. I have to let the momentum, the current, take me wherever God is leading me. Don't fight it, just go.

About a week after this dream I recorded my first audio only podcast. This was huge for me. I previously only used an AI voice to share what I wanted to say, because I was so afraid of everything. I wanted to be used and I wanted to help people, but I had such a hard time stepping out. The

Fear no more

point of the story is this. God goes before you and clears your path, therefore, you have nothing to fear. He is with you and watching over you the whole time. And as much as you feel like swimming back sometimes to where it feels safe, God will cause the current to become so strong, that it makes it that much harder to go back. God doesn't want you to go back, He wants you to move forward with Him. And even though the signs show that up ahead it's going to be a difficult road, He is walking the road with you, and He wont let you drown, even though at times it feels like you are.

Sometimes the things that you are most afraid of, is the exact place that God is leading you.

Releasing the guilt

It took me a really long time to release the guilt that anxiety gave me. I was so mad at myself for being the way I was. I would feel so strong, like I could go outside without feeling fear, but when the time came, I caved. I put myself down a lot for that. It took me a while to realize that it's OK to forgive myself when I mess up, because God forgives me.

I suppose one of the hardest things to do is forgive yourself.

Fear no more

But if you want to move forward, then you can't take unforgiveness with you. Whether it's towards yourself, or towards others.

A little more on forgiving others.

Bless those who persecute you; bless and do not curse. Rejoice with those who rejoice, and weep with those who weep. Be of the same mind toward one another. Do not set your mind on high things, but associate with the humble.
Do not be wise in your own opinion.
Repay no one evil for evil. Have regard for good things in the sight of all men. If it is possible, as much as depends on you, live peaceably with all men. Beloved, do not avenge yourselves, but rather give place to wrath; for it is written, "Vengeance is Mine, I will repay," says the Lord.
Therefore
"If your enemy is hungry, feed him;
If he is thirsty, give him a drink;
For in so doing you will heap coals of fire on his head."

Romans 12:14–20 NKJV

Let me ask you a question. How did Jesus treat those who were mean to Him? Did He scream at them, use His power

Fear no more

to hurt them, or did He lash out at them? No. He did none
of those things.

*For it is commendable if someone bears up under the pain
of unjust suffering because they are conscious of God. But
how is it to your credit if you receive a beating for doing
wrong and endure it? But if you suffer for doing good and
you endure it, this is commendable before God. To this you
were called, because Christ suffered for you, leaving you
an example, that you should follow in his steps.
"He committed no sin,
and no deceit was found in his mouth."
When they hurled their insults at him, he did not retaliate;
when he suffered, he made no threats. Instead, he entrusted
himself to him who judges justly. "He himself bore our
sins" in his body on the cross, so that we might die to sins
and live for righteousness; "by his wounds you have been
healed."*

1 Peter 2:19–24 NIV

I understand how hard it can be to treat someone with
kindness when all they do is hurt you. But the thing is, we
are not called to be like this world nor conform to it.
Instead, we are called to be like Christ. We must remember

that we are not of this world, but of Christ. Therefore, Christ is Who we must imitate.

Jesus showed us that we are to entrust ourselves to God and let Him handle those who have wronged us, however He sees fit.

We are to entrust ourselves to Him who judges justly, even if it's hard at times.

It may be easy to trade insults for insults, but this is not what we are called to do. Not only that, but how could you ever bring others to Jesus Christ, if you aren't showing them what it's like to know Jesus Christ, or what it's like to be like Jesus Christ? This would be equivalent to me cussing, screaming, and belittling someone, and then saying oh, by the way, do you want to know who Jesus Christ is?

We can't lead others to the Light, if we don't exemplify that said Light.

You are the light of the world. A city that is set on a hill cannot be hidden. Nor do they light a lamp and put it under a basket, but on a lampstand, and it gives light to all who are in the house. Let your light so shine before men, that

Fear no more

they may see your good works and glorify your Father in heaven.

Matthew 5:14–16 NKJV

So you have to ask yourself this question. Are you being the light that God calls you to be? Are you setting the stage for others to know Christ, or are you turning them away from Christ with your actions?

It's a lot easier to say that you are a follower of Christ than it is to act on it. Are your actions backing up your words, or are your words empty?

In the same way, faith by itself, if it is not accompanied by action, is dead. But someone will say, "You have faith; I have deeds." Show me your faith without deeds, and I will show you my faith by my deeds. You believe that there is one God. Good! Even the demons believe that — and shudder. You foolish person, do you want evidence that faith without deeds is useless? Was not our father Abraham considered righteous for what he did when he offered his son Isaac on the altar? You see that his faith and his actions were working together, and his faith was made complete by what he did. And the scripture was fulfilled

that says, "Abraham believed God, and it was credited to him as righteousness," and he was called God's friend.

James 2:17–23

In conclusion, I want to say this. I understand how hard it is when someone constantly oppresses you. I understand how hard it is to pray for those who persecute you, oppress you, belittle you, and make you feel bad about yourself. But we are called to be like Jesus.

We have to be better tomorrow than we are today, and we have to overcome evil, with good.

Do not be overcome by evil, but overcome evil with good.

Romans 12:21

I want to also add that God forgives us, therefore, let us forgive others their debts also. See also Matthew 18:21-35.

<u>A little more on forgiving yourself.</u>

You may ask yourself, "Will God really forgive me for all of the things that I have done?"

I want to start by telling you that you don't have to be perfect to come to God.

101

God doesn't want perfect, He wants willing.

You may say, "But you don't know all of the things that I have done, and I have done so many things that I am not proud of. Can God really forgive all of that?"

Simple Answers

The simple answer is yes. Yes He can.

The next question that you may have is this. How would you know?

The simple answer is, the Bible.

The Bible and Paul

Paul is a man in the Bible who you may look at and say the same thing. How could God forgive him?
Before Paul was saved, he searched out God's people to persecute them, and he cast his vote against them.

I too was convinced that I ought to do all that was possible to oppose the name of Jesus of Nazareth. And that is just what I did in Jerusalem. On the authority of the chief priests I put many of the Lord's people in prison, and when they were put to death, I cast my vote against them.

Acts 26:9–10 NIV

102

Paul persecuted believers to their death.

*I am a Jew, born in Tarsus of Cilicia, but brought up in this
city. I studied under Gamaliel and was thoroughly trained
in the law of our ancestors. I was just as zealous for God as
any of you are today. I persecuted the followers of this Way
to their death, arresting both men and women and throwing
them into prison, as the high priest and all the Council can
themselves testify. I even obtained letters from them to their
associates in Damascus, and went there to bring these
people as prisoners to Jerusalem to be punished.*

Acts 22:3–5 NIV

Paul tried to destroy the church of God.

*For you have heard of my former conduct in Judaism, how
I persecuted the church of God beyond measure and tried
to destroy it.*

Galatians 1:13 NKJV

**Paul was a blasphemer, a persecutor, and a violent
man. Yet God showed him mercy.**

*I thank Christ Jesus our Lord, who has given me strength,
that he considered me trustworthy, appointing me to his*

Fear no more

service. Even though I was once a blasphemer and a persecutor and a violent man, I was shown mercy because I acted in ignorance and unbelief. The grace of our Lord was poured out on me abundantly, along with the faith and love that are in Christ Jesus.

Here is a trustworthy saying that deserves full acceptance: Christ Jesus came into the world to save sinners — of whom I am the worst. But for that very reason I was shown mercy so that in me, the worst of sinners, Christ Jesus might display his immense patience as an example for those who would believe in him and receive eternal life. Now to the King eternal, immortal, invisible, the only God, be honor and glory for ever and ever. Amen.

1 Timothy 1:12–17 NIV

God gave us Paul as great example to show us that His grace is for all of us, even those who feel as if they are the worst of sinners.

<u>Why would God even want to forgive me?</u>

Simply because He loves you. And not only does He love you, but He also paid your debt, in full. It's nothing but a lie from the enemy that makes you think that no one could

ever want a sinner like you. That you have done too many things wrong to ever be forgiven. But I'm here to tell you that this couldn't be farther from the truth. God knew exactly who you would be before you were even born. Before God even created this earth, He knew you. He knew all of your mistakes, your regrets, and your failures. Knowing all of this, it was still His will and He was still pleased to call you His own.

Blessed be the God and Father of our Lord Jesus Christ, who has blessed us with every spiritual blessing in the heavenly places in Christ, just as He chose us in Him before the foundation of the world, that we should be holy and without blame before Him in love, having predestined us to adoption as sons by Jesus Christ to Himself, according to the good pleasure of His will, to the praise of the glory of His grace, by which He made us accepted in the Beloved.

Ephesians 1:3-6

God knew everything about you, yet He still died for you. He still went to prepare a place for us so that where He is, we may be also.

105

If God didn't want you, love you, or want to forgive you, would He have given His life to save yours?

For God so loved the world that He gave His only begotten Son, that whoever believes in Him should not perish but have everlasting life.

John 3:16 NKJV

<u>The weight that you feel</u>

That weight you feel, the weight of all your sins, was already paid for at the cross. This means that once you take the correct step of accepting Jesus as your Lord and Savior, once you confess with your mouth that Jesus is Lord, and believe in your heart that God raised Him from the dead, you will be saved.

If you declare with your mouth, "Jesus is Lord," and believe in your heart that God raised him from the dead, you will be saved.

Romans 10:9 NIV

Fear no more

You will be saved.

Saved from your sins, from your guilt, and from your shame. Your sins, nailed to the cross.

He forgave us all our sins, having canceled the charge of our legal indebtedness, which stood against us and condemned us; he has taken it away, nailing it to the cross.

Colossians 2:13–14 NIV

This can only happen…

This can only happen if you choose to accept Jesus. If you choose to believe that Jesus is Lord, and believe in your heart that He died and that God raised Him from the dead. And if you haven't taken this important step yet, and you want the forgiveness that God offers you, if you want the insurmountable love that He offers you, tell Him.

<u>But I don't know how to pray.</u>

That's OK.

I can help you with that.

Please pray this prayer with me.

107

Dear God,

I come before you today, declaring that Jesus is Lord. I confess with my mouth that Jesus died, and that You raised Him from the dead. I want to live my life for You God. Change me and make me more like Jesus. With this prayer, I know that I have now been forgiven of all of my sins. I know that no matter how bad I have sinned, the blood that You shed for me on the cross covered those sins. Thank You for the love that You have shown me. Today I make the choice to follow You. Please guide me and show me how to do that. In Jesus name I pray, Amen.

So from now on we regard no one from a worldly point of view. Though we once regarded Christ in this way, we do so no longer. Therefore, if anyone is in Christ, the new creation has come: The old has gone, the new is here! All this is from God, who reconciled us to himself through Christ and gave us the ministry of reconciliation: that God was reconciling the world to himself in Christ, not counting people's sins against them. And he has committed to us the message of reconciliation. We are therefore Christ's ambassadors, as though God were making his appeal through us. We implore you on Christ's behalf:

Be reconciled to God. God made him who had no sin to be sin for us, so that in him we might become the righteousness of God.

2 Corinthians 5:16–21 NIV

I am so proud of you.

If you prayed that prayer, I am so proud of you! The road ahead is not an easy one, but God will be walking it with you every step of the way. No matter what comes against you, don't lose your faith in God. The devil will try whatever he can to get you to stop believing. Stand firm in your faith and resist the devil.

Therefore submit to God. Resist the devil and he will flee from you. Draw near to God and He will draw near to you.

James 4:7-8 NKJV

For some more info on becoming a new believer, please visit my podcast URL below titled, "Dear new Christians." https://youtu.be/oj5SEfntSTc

What now?

I cannot stress how important it is for you to read God's word. If you don't have a Bible, that's OK. There are free

109

Fear no more

apps that you can read from at no cost to you. I recommend YouVersion. If you don't have a phone, it's also on desktop at Bible.com. I also recommend starting in the book of Matthew, however, if you feel led to start somewhere else, that's OK too. There are a total of 66 books in the Bible. I recommend the NKJV and NIV versions. NKJV has better accuracy than the NIV, and the NIV is easier to understand. I like to use both, but you can definitely start with the NIV for easier reading.

Be Careful.

Be careful with what version of the Bible you choose to read, as there are some that are incorrect in their teachings. For example, NEVER use the New World Translation version (NWT). It has many inaccuracies. Remember that the Bible version you read does matter.

In Conclusion

I pray that out of his glorious riches he may strengthen you with power through his Spirit in your inner being, so that Christ may dwell in your hearts through faith. And I pray that you, being rooted and established in love, may have power, together with all the Lord's holy people, to grasp

110

*how wide and long and high and deep is the love of Christ,
and to know this love that surpasses knowledge — that you
may be filled to the measure of all the fullness of God.*

Ephesians 3:16-19 NIV

Let's continue with our topic on anxiety.

Even though it may feel that what you are going through couldn't possibly be used for good, it can and it will. Whatever the enemy meant for evil, God meant it for your good.

Then Joseph said to his brothers, "Come close to me." When they had done so, he said, "I am your brother Joseph, the one you sold into Egypt! And now, do not be distressed and do not be angry with yourselves for selling me here, because it was to save lives that God sent me ahead of you. For two years now there has been famine in the land, and for the next five years there will be no plowing and reaping. But God sent me ahead of you to preserve for you a remnant on earth and to save your lives by a great deliverance.
"So then, it was not you who sent me here, but God.

Genesis 45:4-8 NIV

Fear no more

You intended to harm me, but God intended it for good to accomplish what is now being done, the saving of many lives.

Genesis 50:20 NIV

Therefore, we can conclude the fact that whatever harm the enemy meant to cause you from this, God meant it for good. And guess what?

God always wins.

<u>We can overcome any obstacles we face.</u>

Why? Because Jesus overcame the world, and so can we.

"I have told you these things, so that in me you may have peace. In this world you will have trouble. But take heart! I have overcome the world."

John 16:33 NIV

This scripture proves that we will have trouble in this world, but it also proves that we can overcome it.

So yes, in this world we will have many troubles, but take heart, because Jesus has overcome the world.

If we are walking through this life alone, then we could

113

never overcome this world, but with Jesus, we can overcome anything.

He lives in us, and we live in Him. Therefore, we have the strength that we need to overcome it as well.

Not by our own strength, but through the strength of Jesus Christ who lives in us. As we abide in the Vine, the Vine abides in us, and as we draw near to God, God draws near to us.

Through Him, we have all the strength that we will ever need. For when we are weak, then we are strong.

But he said to me, "My grace is sufficient for you, for my power is made perfect in weakness." Therefore I will boast all the more gladly about my weaknesses, so that Christ's power may rest on me. That is why, for Christ's sake, I delight in weaknesses, in insults, in hardships, in persecutions, in difficulties. For when I am weak, then I am strong.

2 Corinthians 12:9–10 NIV

Fear no more

Chapter 22
My advice

What advice can I give you?

Here are a few of the many things that I have learned along the way. I truly hope and pray that they will help you as well.

#1 Are you reading the Bible?

Staying in God's word is crucial to overcoming anxiety. I get that sometimes it may be hard to concentrate when you are in the middle of a panic attack, but trust me, this is a must. If I didn't lean on God while I was at my worst, I wouldn't be where I am today. Therefore, make sure that you are reading your Bible, daily.

Keep this Book of the Law always on your lips; meditate on it day and night, so that you may be careful to do everything written in it. Then you will be prosperous and successful.

Joshua 1:8 NIV

Fear no more

Blessed is the one who does not walk in step with the wicked or stand in the way that sinners take or sit in the company of mockers, but whose delight is in the law of the LORD, and who meditates on his law day and night. That person is like a tree planted by streams of water, which yields its fruit in season and whose leaf does not wither—whatever they do prospers.

Psalm 1:1-3 NIV

Always remember that God didn't just give us the scriptures to read them, but to follow them and live them out.

There is no replacement to reading God's word. Listening to sermons is great too, but reading is essential. Just you and God. There should be no distractions if possible. Give God your **full** attention. Why? Because He deserves it, and because He truly does love spending time with you.

#2 Stop calling it MY anxiety!

I used to make this mistake, and I still sometimes catch myself doing it. I would say things like MY anxiety, or I have anxiety.

DON'T CLAIM IT!

It's not yours, you don't want it to be yours, and it's not going to be yours. Why? Because you don't belong to the anxiety or fear, you belong to God. God didn't give us a spirit of fear, but of power, love, and a sound mind, and that's exactly what you need to claim. A sound mind.

For God has not given us a spirit of fear, but of power and of love and of a sound mind.

2 Timothy 1:7 NKJV

#3 Replace the negative with the positive.

Every single time that a negative thought pops in your head, replace it with a positive thought. As a matter of fact, replace it with two! I know it's not easy when you are in the middle of a panic attack to focus on anything but the panic, but even though it may be hard at first, keep trying.

Eventually, it will get easier.

Finally, brethren, whatever things are true, whatever things are noble, whatever things are just, whatever things are pure, whatever things are lovely, whatever things are of good report, if there is any virtue and if there is anything praiseworthy — meditate on these things. The things which you learned and received and heard and saw in me, these

117

#4 Do you remember how I mentioned that you need to be in God's word?

When I was at the height of my anxiety, I realized something that really helped me with the panic attacks and anxious thoughts. The moment that you get an attack, and I mean literally the same second, grab your Bible and read.

DO NOT STOP UNTIL THE ATTACK GOES AWAY.

Sometimes I would read and the attacks would keep coming, but I would try my best to keep going and not stop. Remember, don't stop reading. Even if it takes hours and even if it takes all day. Resist the negative and focus on the positive. Focus on God and His word, and those anxious thoughts will flee from you.

I look at it like this. As we walk through this life, the devil will always be there to try and tempt us to be anxious, worried, fearful, etc. But even though he may be there, so is God. And it's up to you to choose what you focus on. And although it may be hard at first, the more you focus your attention on God, the easier it gets. Remember that

Fear no more

God always provides a way out of an attack from the enemy, but it's up to you to take it.

No temptation has overtaken you except what is common to mankind. And God is faithful; he will not let you be tempted beyond what you can bear. But when you are tempted, he will also provide a way out so that you can endure it.

1 Corinthians 10:13 NIV

I made a podcast episode that I believe may help you. The URL is below. It's titled, "Trust Him."

https://www.youtube.com/watch?v=LNxxGDCWRIg

#5 Worship through it.

There is something really powerful about praising God in the midst of a storm. Lifting your hands in full submission to God, regardless of what you are going through and regardless of what you are feeling. Not only does He deserve all of the glory and praise, but worshiping in the middle of a storm is a great way to overcome an anxiety attack.

Let me explain.

Do you know the scripture above that I wrote? The one that

119

says to focus on the good and praiseworthy? You won't find anything in this entire universe that is more praiseworthy and good than our God. So give Him all of your attention, and trust Him to give you the peace that you need to fight through those anxious thoughts.

"Come to me, all you who are weary and burdened, and I will give you rest. Take my yoke upon you and learn from me, for I am gentle and humble in heart, and you will find rest for your souls. For my yoke is easy and my burden is light."

Matthew 11:28-30 NIV

If you notice the scripture above, there is an action that is first done on your part. And that action is "*Come to me*". Therefore, come to Jesus and let Him give you the peace that you seek.

#6 Pray.

This may seem like a no-brainer, but it can be easy to forget in the middle of a panic attack. So remember to pray. Ask God for His strength, ask God for His help, and thank Him for all that He has done and all that He will do. While you are thanking Him, thank Him for helping you

overcome what you are facing. Thank Him for the things that you can't yet see, because you know that one day you will see them, because God is faithful, good, and just. And if you find yourself in a moment when you are so distraught that you don't know what to pray, just talk to Him. Ask the Holy Spirit to guide you and help you pray.

In the same way, the Spirit helps us in our weakness. We do not know what we ought to pray for, but the Spirit himself intercedes for us through wordless groans. And he who searches our hearts knows the mind of the Spirit, because the Spirit intercedes for God's people in accordance with the will of God.

Romans 8:26-27 NIV

#7 Claim the victory before you even see it.

Death and life are in the power of the tongue, And those who love it will eat its fruit.

Proverbs 18:21

What you choose to speak over yourself matters. These scriptures affirm that what we choose to say and believe about ourselves makes all the difference.

For as he thinks in his heart, so is he.

Proverbs 23:7

121

Fear no more

You can speak life over yourself, or you can speak death. You can speak victory, or you can speak defeat.

The choice ultimately lies in your hands. But remember, if you are constantly thinking that you will never get better, then that's speaking defeat.

Declare the victory before your eyes even see the victory.

For in this hope we were saved. But hope that is seen is no hope at all. Who hopes for what they already have? But if we hope for what we do not yet have, we wait for it patiently.

Romans 8:24-25 NIV

#8 He will never leave your side.

Sometimes when you are in the middle of a panic attack, it can be really hard to feel God's presence. This is because you can become so caught up in the fear that everything else looks blurry, but trust me, He is right there with you.

Whether you feel Him or not, He is there. He does love you, and He does care about what you are going through.

#9 It may feel like it, but fear DOESN'T protect you.

I used to think that the fear was protecting me, however, God showed me differently. Here is what God showed me.

At one point in my journey, I felt as if God was putting it on my heart to do what Joshua did in the Bible. He marched around the city seven times. One time a day for six days, and then seven times on the seventh day. On the seventh day they gave a large shout and the walls of the city crumbled and fell down. Joshua and the army attacked and overtook the city and won. This secure city that their adversaries had up was so secure and fortified, yet the powerful and mighty hand of God crumbled it in an instant. All because by faith, God's people believed in Him. Believed in God's deliverance. By faith they marched, believing that the enemy would be delivered into their hands. By faith they believed this, and God delivered them. I was hoping to do the same on this walk. Here is what I wrote about this hope in my notes, when I chose to do this walk around my house.

My hope is that what feels like these fortified walls inside of me, start to crumble with every walk. The foundation of fear, anxiety, doubt, etc, start giving way until on that

Fear no more

seventh day they utterly crumble and dissipate. Just like the walls of Jericho, the army by faith marched around a wall that they could not take down themselves, and entrusted themselves to a loving Father, this I also do. I claim victory over this war waging inside of me, not by my might, but God's. Because the walls are too strong for me, but God, there is nothing that my God can't do. With His mighty hand He will deliver me because He loves me. By faith I trust God and believe that this battle is not mine, but God's. By faith I will move from fear to faith. By faith, my wonderful loving Father will deliver me. By faith, God will crumble what does not belong inside of me, and what is left will be the strongest, fortified foundation and building that I have yet seen in me. By faith, I believe.

You will not have to fight this battle. Take up your positions; stand firm and see the deliverance the LORD will give you

2 Chronicles 20:17 NIV

<u>The walk</u>

During this walk God taught me something. When I was doing my Jericho walk around the house, I was afraid. If a

car passed by I had to tell myself to keep going, but I still felt anxious. On the last day of my walk I was so scared. You have to understand that just me being outside was a HUGE battlefield. My husband had done the walk with me for six days after I asked him to. He wanted to support me so he said yes. However, on this last day I felt like I was supposed to finish the walk with just me and God. I talked to my husband and he would do the first walk with me and I would do the other six. This would complete the seven and final laps around the house. When my husband walked with me it helped ease the anxiety some knowing that he was there, but I felt it on my heart to finish the race with my eyes fully on God. I was scared, but I also knew that I had to do it. As bad as I wanted him to walk with me, and as bad as I wanted him to at least stand there as I went around, I knew what I felt I had to do. I was afraid, but giving up was not an option. I asked God if He was willing to have no cars pass by, so it was easier for me, but if that wasn't His will then I wanted Him to do whatever was best in His eyes, because He knew better than me. So going into this, I wasn't sure if I would face packed roads or little to no one. As much as I wanted bare roads, I wanted God's will more. So we started the walk. The first lap my husband

Fear no more

did with me and then waited inside for me to finish. On the first lap an animal ran passed us, but I refused to stop and see what it was, I had to keep going. First lap done. My husband went inside. I wasn't alone though, God was with me. I walked fast. I didn't run, but I was power walking. The air conditioner for the house came on the second that I passed it. Loud noises scared me. The noise was so loud that it startled me, but I couldn't stop. I had to keep going. So the first lap was done, no cars, second lap, no cars, third lap, no cars. I was out of breath from how fast I was walking, however, I had to go fast because I was scared. Fourth lap, no cars. Can't breathe but I have to push. Power walked the fifth lap, no cars, the sixth lap, no cars. As I reached the side of the house, I was getting ready for the seventh and final lap soon. I then feel this pull telling me to finish the last walk with me and God without power walking. To take my time this last lap. However, the fear gripped me and I said to myself "I can't, I have to keep going." Then I get to the back of the house. I say it again, "slow down. I need to slow down." I tell myself "I can't, I have to finish, I have to go fast. No cars have been by and I have to go fast." You see, I thought that if I went fast, it would prevent the cars from passing because I was

hurrying. As I get to the other side of the house before reaching the front, a car passes by. I get anxious but I had to keep going. After I was done and I had time to think, this became a HUGE lesson for me. I believe that voice was the Holy Spirit trying to tell me to slow down, but the fear clouded that voice. I was so scared that I let fear override everything else, and in turn I was unintentionally allowing it to cloud the voice of God. We may feel as if fear protects us when we have anxiety, but it doesn't. The only thing that can truly protect us is God. The fear led me to believe that if I went fast, no cars would come because nothing has come yet and one might come soon, so walk fast, don't stop. But the thing is, you can't see what's up ahead, only God can. It was foolish of me to think that just because I was walking fast I could avoid the cars. Looking back at this moment, I see God trying to not only protect me from having anxiety on that last walk, but I believe that He was showing me that I may not be able to see ahead, but He does. I just need to trust Him and believe that He will protect me. And I mean truly believe. Not letting fear dictate how fast I walk. Not letting fear dictate if I go to the store or to the doctors. God showed me that day that the fear was actually bringing me outside of God's will,

because I was so focused on giving into the fear to avoid it, that I wasn't allowing God's voice to be above that said fear, and this was a HUGE mistake on my part.

I have come to realize that you can't listen to both voices at once. Therefore, you have to ask yourself this question.

Are you afraid, or do you believe?

The Bible is clear that we can not serve two masters, therefore, you must choose to either allow the fear to guide you, or allow God to guide you. You can't have both.

Remember that a life driven by fear is a life in captivity. A life lived and walked by faith in God, is a life in freedom. Which one will you choose?

#10 Breathe.

Yes, breathe. I know what you may be thinking. Of course I am breathing! If I weren't breathing would I still be alive? Seriously though. Breathe. One breath in, one breath out. Slow and steady.

At one point I was doing breath prayers during an attack. You take a scripture, you make it yours, and you breathe it in. Here are ones that I personally made and used. I based

them off of scripture, and then said them as if I was saying them to myself and God. I will put the scriptures that I based these off of after, so you can see the actual scripture that goes with it.

Breath in: Your presence goes with me
Breath out: and gives me rest
Breath in: Lord, You are with me
Breath out: wherever I go
Breath in: The Lord comforts His people
Breath out: and has compassion on His afflicted ones.
Breath in: Lord, Your unfailing love
Breath out: is my greatest comfort
Breath in: I remember Your word
Breath out: and find comfort in it.
Breath in: I am not afraid
Breath out: for You will save me
Breath in: Wherever I go, Lord
Breath out: You are there
Breath in: I cast my anxieties on You
Breath out: because You care about me
Breath in: I hold firmly to hope
Breath out: because You are faithful

Fear no more

The scriptures that I based these off of are below.

And He said, "My Presence will go with you, and I will give you rest."

Exodus 33:14 NKJV

Have I not commanded you? Be strong and of good courage; do not be afraid, nor be dismayed, for the Lord your God is with you wherever you go."

Joshua 1:9 NKJV

Sing, O heavens! Be joyful, O earth! And break out in singing, O mountains! For the LORD has comforted His people, And will have mercy on His afflicted.

Isaiah 49:13 NKJV

May your unfailing love be my comfort, according to your promise to your servant.

Psalm 119:76 NIV

I remember, LORD, your ancient laws, and I find comfort in them.

Psalm 119:52 NIV

Fear no more

Do not be afraid of them, for I am with you and will rescue you," declares the Lord.

Jeremiah 1:8 NIV

If I go up to the heavens, you are there; if I make my bed in the depths, you are there. If I rise on the wings of the dawn, if I settle on the far side of the sea, even there your hand will guide me, your right hand will hold me fast.

Psalm 139:8-10 NIV

Cast all your anxiety on him because he cares for you.

1 Peter 5:7 NIV

Let us hold fast the confession of our hope without wavering, for He who promised is faithful.

Hebrews 10:23 NKJV

These are just some of the ones that I personally used. Hopefully they can help you as well. Also, here are a few additional ones that I thought of.

131

Breath in: I have all the power I need
Breath out: to overcome this fear.
Breath in: I can conquer this fear
Breath out: because His perfect love casts it out
Breath in: I was given authority
Breath out: to defeat this
Breath in: I am safe in Your hands Lord
Breath out: nothing will hurt me

There is no fear in love; but perfect love casts out fear, because fear involves torment. But he who fears has not been made perfect in love.

1 John 4:18

Yet in all these things we are more than conquerors through Him who loved us.

Romans 8:37

Behold, I give you the authority to trample on serpents and scorpions, and over all the power of the enemy, and nothing shall by any means hurt you.

Luke 10:19

Fear no more

Remember this.

The enemy wants you to look at the fear, so you miss out on what God has in store for you. If you are too busy looking at the anxiety, you will have a harder time noticing what God is trying to show you.

It's difficult to look at something in front of you, while your eyes are looking behind you.

Don't become so consumed with the fear, that you allow it to rob you of your future.

Scriptures

Another thing that I have found comfort in is Psalm 91. Whenever you feel fear, read Psalm 91. It is a wonderful reminder that you are safe, loved, and protected. Another one that I love is Psalm 23.

Below is the URL to one of my podcasts that I feel may help you as well.

https://youtu.be/0yIXuAUTJJg

Fear no more

Not a race.

These are just a few of the many things that you can do to help you overcome a panic and anxiety attack.

I won't sit here and tell you that it's easy, because it's far from it. I am years into this fight, but I am so grateful to be able to tell you that it does get better, and it does get easier. At first it may feel like you are taking one step forward just to take ten steps back.

It's OK, you will get there when you get there. Remember, it's not a race, it's a journey.

Try to remember.

Your main focus should be on God. Keep your eyes on God. He will never leave you, never forsake you, and never fail you. Trust Him to get you through this. As I said before, God is faithful, and He is walking through this with you. Trust Him.

Know therefore that the Lord your God is God; he is the faithful God, keeping his covenant of love to a thousand generations of those who love him and keep his commandments.

Deuteronomy 7:9 NIV

Fear no more

Chapter 24
Your authority

If you are living in constant fear, I have something to say to you.

Dear child, don't you know who you are?

It took me a long time to realize who I was in Christ. I allowed fear to tell me what I could and couldn't do for so long, that I started thinking that it was in control. I avoided things just because it was scary. I came to learn that avoiding what was scary didn't help me, it only hurt me. As an example, I listened to fear tell me not to go in the front yard, then it turned into the backyard too, then the screen room outside, then the living room, kitchen, and eventually fear crept in even sitting in a chair in my room.

The more I gave fear, the more it required of me.

I want to share a scripture with you below.

Fear no more

When He had come to the other side, to the country of the Gergesenes, there met Him two demon-possessed men, coming out of the tombs, exceedingly fierce, so that no one could pass that way. And suddenly they cried out, saying, "What have we to do with You, Jesus, You Son of God? Have You come here to torment us before the time?" Now a good way off from them there was a herd of many swine feeding. So the demons begged Him, saying, "If You cast us out, permit us to go away into the herd of swine." And He said to them, "Go." So when they had come out, they went into the herd of swine. And suddenly the whole herd of swine ran violently down the steep place into the sea, and perished in the water.

Matthew 8:28-32

These people thought that the demons were so fierce, yet who did they cower before? Jesus Christ. And Who lives inside of you?

I also want to point something else out. The demons were begging Jesus to let them go into the pigs. Why is that? Because He had authority over them, and because they could do NOTHING apart from what Jesus allowed them to do.

Fear no more

I'm about to tell you something, are you ready?

That fear that is trying to assert its authority over you is a liar. The fear has it backwards. You have ALL authority over that fear, NOT the other way around.

This authority was given to you by God, and no one can override it. By you allowing the fear to circumvent your life, it's like a King of a nation giving all of his authority to his child. That child then turns around and gives it to a person who is an enemy to the kingdom, one who wants to destroy it, and has no status in it.

The fear has an end, you don't. The fear will one day perish along with satan and his demons. Why wait until that day, when you have the authority to stop it now?

I know, it sometimes takes a while. I'm not saying that it's going to be easy, but I am saying that it's possible. It's easy to say that you will just deal with it the rest of your life, however, God never intended this to be so. God wants to see you healed from your afflictions. Start claiming your authority over every mountain that tries to exalt itself above what you know to be true. That you are a child of the Most High God. Your Father is the King of Kings. And as

Fear no more

His child, you have been given all power, all authority, and all dominion over satan and his lies. You are the Kings child! Don't EVER allow satan, who isn't even a part of the kingdom, diminish you and the role that you have. God has plans for you. Assert your authority over that fear no matter how long it takes, and NEVER GIVE UP!

If you choose to keep going, if you choose to never give up, and if you choose to assert your authority over that fear, anxiety, etc, it's equivalent to tearing wallpaper off of a wall. It's hard, it's frustrating, it takes time, it looks like you're not getting anywhere, and at first it looks like you have so long to go, but with every tear you become closer and closer to what it's meant to look like. You start seeing glimpses of joy again. For years I didn't see this. I was always sad, always crying, and my joy seemed to be so distant that I couldn't even remember what joy felt like. However, every step that God led me on, kept chipping away at that wall, little by little, and eventually after many years, God helped me find joy again. And I know that if you keep going, you will see it too. I don't say this just to say it, I say this because I lived it. God, He is faithful, kind, and good. And I hope that you choose to keep pressing on with Him, and I know that God does too.

Fear no more

Chapter 25
Focus

To close, I want to say this. Overcoming obstacles in this life can be really difficult, but they are never impossible.

Instead of focusing on the obstacles, try to focus on the Obstacle Mover, and focus on the end result.

I mean this in two parts. The first part is this. Whatever pain you feel now does have a purpose. You may not see it, you may not feel it, and you may even at times have trouble believing it, but it's true.

God always has a reason and a purpose for all that He does, and all that He allows.

Remember the pain that Joseph and Job endured? It all had a purpose. Look at the life of Esther. The Bible tells us that she had no father nor mother. Mordecai had taken her as his own daughter when her father and mother died. It can be quick to look at this situation and ask why she had to suffer this way. Why she had to endure the loss of both her father

Fear no more

and her mother. Yet this tragedy was what brought her to Mordecai, which then brought her to being queen, which then brought her to help save many Jews at the request of Mordecai, and ultimately the request of God. One can look at this situation as terrible and sad, or one can look at it as preordained by God for the saving of many people. Joseph, he endured much in his life. However, what he endured brought him to where he was meant to be. God used him to help save many people from a famine that struck the land. Jesus, He suffered a painful death. Looking at all that He endured on this earth is heartbreaking. As painful as this was, Jesus's pain did have a purpose. One that we will NEVER deserve.

God has a purpose for everything. A purpose for the sun, a purpose for the moon, a purpose for your pain, and a purpose for your life.

Don't allow your pain to overcome the truth that God is not finished with you yet.

And remember, your pain will not only turn out for your good, but also for His glory.

being confident of this, that he who began a good work in you will carry it on to completion until the day of Christ Jesus.

Philippians 1:6 NIV

Fear no more

<u>Don't fear</u>

Don't fear what you face, instead, believe that what you face is the path that you must take in order to reach the purpose in which God made you for.

Think of the anxiety or whatever it is that you are facing as the floor of a bridge, and your faith as the railing. You need to cross over the bridge, trampling on and through the anxiety and problems, as you hold onto your faith. Don't let go of your faith. The bridge may look and feel scary to cross, but you have to cross it to get to where you are going, to where God is leading you. If you turn back and choose not to cross the bridge, then you will never get to see the beauty that awaits you on the other side.

Be grateful for the bridge. Even if it's a painful one.

Because when you reach the other side of it, you will see that although it was a long and painful bridge, it was the only bridge that could get you to where God wanted you to go.

These words may seem hard to grasp at the moment, but in time, I pray that that you will see them in its entirety.

Fear no more

I leave you with these words.

And the God of all grace, who called you to his eternal glory in Christ, after you have suffered a little while, will himself restore you and make you strong, firm and steadfast.

1 Peter 5:10

**I know that the pain you bear is hard, but give it to Me, and I will bear it for you.
Everything is going to be OK. Trust Me.**

Fear no more

The drawing on the cover

<u>The meaning of the drawing on the cover</u>

Forget-me-nots
Because God will never forget about you

Three flowers on each stem
Father, Son, and Spirit

Water in the vase
Saturated, watered, and filled by the Holy Spirit

Cracks in the vase
Because we all feel a little broken sometimes

Red filled cracks
Jesus mends and fills those cracks. Those spots in our heart that feel so broken, He heals them. And what does He heal them with? His unfailing love. The love of God. I filled them with red because yes, the color of love, but more so, because of the blood that was shed for us at the cross. What greater love than this? Than the One who laid down His life for us, His friends. Jesus's blood tells those cracks, "It is finished."

The table at the bottom

So often we feel like if we let go, we will fall. What we fail to remember at times is this. You were never holding yourself up in the first place, God is. Always has, is, and will be God. Therefore, even if you feel as if you're falling, the truth is, you are held. And that, by God Himself.

The top part of the vase that goes through part of the stem at the top

This was a mistake. And rather than correct it, I chose to accept that it happened and learn from it. I just started doing drawings like this, and when you first start something, it's much easier to mess up because you are learning. It's just like life. This is the first time we are all doing life. We are all learning as we go, and sometimes we seem to forget this. When a child messes up, we correct them, but we also know that they are still learning. Therefore, go easy on yourself, and rather than beat yourself up over it, learn from it and try to do better next time. Remember that we are not perfect, but thankfully God is. He understands that we aren't always going to get things right. And guess what? He loves you anyway!

The crack and soil at the bottom

Sometimes we spend so much time hiding inside of this earthen vessel. We assume that if we show people our pain, our hurt, and our struggles, we will be less than. However, the most beautiful parts come from within us, from the places that people don't usually see. Think about all of the beauty that God has placed within us. The Holy Spirit is within us. This is beautiful. All of our organs and the things that God so intricately made, the things that allow us to breathe and continue to give us life are all on the inside of us. This is beautiful. Jesus Christ is in us, and us in Him. Who are we that God is so mindful of us, that He allows someone as small as dust to be His temple? This is beautiful. Jesus, He died and rose again, allowing those who chose to believe to also be one with the Father who is within us. This is beautiful. Remember that your scars, your pain, and the things that hurt you, the things that you tape off on the inside, help others see that even in the pain, there is beauty. There is healing. This, is beautiful.

The roots

The healing that I spoke of, it's only in Jesus Christ that we find this. In Him all things hold together. When you choose

to be brave and allow others to see your painful moments, the struggles and the trials, you are also allowing them to see the One who stood by your side through every bit of it, mending, fixing, repairing, comforting, and loving you. When they see the struggles, when they see the inside of you, they also see the roots. They see Jesus Christ.

The clay pot

Remember that we aren't the potter, we are the clay. We always try so hard to make ourselves into something. We fail to realize that this isn't our job. God already has a preordained plan for you, and He doesn't need your help trying to figure out where your place is, as He already knows. Your ultimate place is with Him, and He also has things that He has in store for you in this life. If you are having trouble figuring out where God wants you, ask Him. And even if He says wait, remember that we are to keep our eyes on God and obey. Even when it hurts, even when it's hard, and even when God says to wait. And even though the molding process hurts, a lot, always try to remember that it's always for your good, and God's glory. If you're going through something, God has a purpose for allowing it. You may not see it now, but in time, you will.

Fear no more

The plain background

There is still more to your story. God isn't finished with you yet. How do I know? You're still breathing aren't you? God is still preparing, still painting, still parting, and still working. If you give up now, you won't get to see the beautiful backdrop that He has planned for you. And how do I know it will be good? Because we serve a good God.

Thank you so much for reading this book and being a part
of my journey!

Fear no more

The one always matters

The one always matters